GOD
AND
MARRIAGE

by
Geoffrey W. Bromiley

Grand Rapids
WILLIAM B. EERDMANS PUBLISHING COMPANY

To my wife Isabel,
our daughters Katherine and Ruth,
and their husbands James and Timothy

Copyright © 1980 by Wm. B. Eerdmans Publishing Co.
255 Jefferson Ave. S.E., Grand Rapids, Mich. 49503

All rights reserved

Printed in the United States of America

Library of Congress Cataloging in Publication Data:

Bromiley, Geoffrey William.
    God and marriage.

      1. Marriage.   I. Title.
BV835.B726   261.8′358   80-17566
ISBN 0-8028-1851-X

Contents

Preface

THIS study is intentionally unpretentious in nature and purpose. It attempts no profound or detailed scholarly investigation of marriage but simply takes a look at God's relation to it in holy scripture. It enters into no dialogue with other writers or teachers but aims at a positive individual statement. It tries to avoid presuppositions — if one can really do this so late in Christian history! — and to focus on a plain and orderly presentation of the available data. It enters into no investigation or evaluation of the historical background or development of the human thinking involved, although naturally a certain historical progression emerges with the unfolding exposition. It does not press practical references or applications, which in many instances will be obvious without extensive or obtrusive commentary. It rests on the conviction — here perhaps is a presupposition — that in virtue of its divine as well as human origin and use, scripture forms, as God speaks through it, the supreme rule of faith and conduct, so that in marriage, too, it has a pertinence beyond that of any other authority. It recognizes that, while none of us can see things precisely as God sees them, to study scripture as the word of God is to get a glimpse of God's view. It aims, then, to present marriage as it stands in the light of God's own word and action, so that we may better conform our own concept and practice of marriage to the divine will and work and goal.

Introduction

NOT another book on marriage? The question is a good one. The world seems to be full of books on marriage. Writing one might almost be called a fashion. People come at the subject from all conceivable angles. They deluge the married and the unmarried with information and advice of every type. They do so whether they themselves are married, divorced, divorced and remarried, or single. If books on marriage could ensure good marriages, no marriages in history would be better than today's.

Unhappily, it does not work out that way. Not only do we have such a pile of books on marriage that one more might seem to be unnecessary, but those we already have seem to make very little difference to marriage as fact in distinction from marriage as theory. Marriages run into difficulties — for many people insuperable difficulties — on every hand. Dissolutions and remarriages abound. Various substitutes — living together, trial marriages, limited unions — threaten to replace authentic marriage. Even in Christian circles — in the most orthodox and biblical Christian circles — the spate of books is failing to arrest the more powerful counterflow of failure and change.

What is to be expected, then, of another book? No matter how wise or witty or true, can it hope to bring about a decisive turn in the course of events? Can it do what all the other books so far have fairly obviously failed to do? Can it make any significant difference at all either one way or the other?

Realistically, the chance of exerting widescale influence is obviously not very high. All the same, every contribution can do something. Many people want as well as need guidance in a confusing situation. Others need confirmation. Others who have gone the way of failure seek reorientation. Many needs may already be met at the individual level by one or another of the existing books. Elsewhere, however, a gap may still exist. Hence "another book" can play a role of limited, if by no means universal, significance.

But there is more to it than that. Books on marriage approach it from many angles — most of them valid. Few of these works, however, are decidedly and distinctively theological. Theology has for many people a forbidding sound. It suggests theory, and the very last person to deal with the down-to-earth practicalities of marriage is surely the theorist. Books on marriage tend, then, to stress the practical elements and to go easy on theology. In so doing they make a serious mistake. True theology has the most direct and crucial practical implications. Even in relation to people who are struggling with foundering marriages — or precisely in relation to such people — a theological book on marriage might be the best possible book. There is still a need for such a book.

In reality does not a theology of marriage involve an exposition of the biblical materials on the subject? Indeed it does, for theology has to build with the blocks of revelation which God has given and gives us in and through holy scripture. But do not the Christian books on marriage present the biblical materials in either summarized or more extended form, so that all that is meant by a theology of marriage already exists in these works? As regards the main question, the answer is "yes." Christian books undoubtedly contain much information on what the Bible says about marriage. A new study will not turn up many new facts or shed any very new light on the facts already presented. Nevertheless, this does not rule out the need for "another book." For the answer to the inference made from the question is a definite "no." It does not follow from the presence of biblical expositions that "all that is meant by a theology of marriage already exists in these works."

Why not? A first reason has to do with the way in which the biblical data are handled. For some writers and readers the biblical material has the rank of an ideal for which we are all to aim but which we cannot realistically hope to achieve, since the pressures and complexities of life prove too strong not only for non-Christians but for Christians too. Others connect the biblical statements very closely to their original historical and cultural background. These statements, they say, have normative rank in their own setting but their force and applicability vary with changed and changing cultures and settings. As scripture itself conforms to its own age and place, so it may be permissible for us to conform in some measure to our own age and place. Others argue that the directives of scripture cannot in any case constitute imperatives for Christians who live under grace and not under law. These directives may accuse us but they cannot order us about. The freedom of the children of God implies that they may take note of biblical injunctions, but in marriage as in all else they must always act according to the special guidance of the Holy Spirit and the requirement of the higher commandment of love, using perhaps the "right to happiness" as a more utilitarian norm. The necessities of life in a fallen world impose choices not only between the good and the bad but also between the bad and the less bad in which simple observance of the directives of scripture is impossible. A common feature in all these ways of handling the Bible is the assumption that it offers us a "law of marriage" which cannot be kept for various reasons and is thus to be evaded in various ways. But a law of marriage differs decisively from a theology of marriage.

The second reason why we should not conclude that all that is meant by a theology of marriage exists in biblical expositions of the topic depends on the distinction that must be made between God and the Bible. Everybody can see this distinction. We call the Bible God-inspired. In that sense we can even describe it as "divine." We can equate it with God's word or relate it to God's revelation. Yet the Bible is not God. We can learn about God in it. We have to do so. God reveals himself in and through the Bible. He speaks in and through it. Yet the Bible does not replace God. He has not just given us the Bible and left us to it. He himself is still the one with whom we have to deal. And this, after all, is what theology is all about. As the term itself tells us, God stands at the center. Even as we consult holy scripture, we are really consulting

God himself in his self-revelation as he came and comes to us through holy scripture. God indeed says what scripture says, but this does not imply a direct equation of God and scripture.

What does this have to do with the present issue? Simply put, it means that although an account of the biblical teaching on marriage may be a theology of marriage, it will not necessarily be so. Why not? Because no theology of marriage or of anything else arises if the teaching is abstracted from God himself, if God himself is not present at the heart and center in his own relation to the topic. A theology of marriage does not consist of a mere recital of what the biblical texts have to say about it. It consists of the relating of marriage to God, or of God to marriage, as he himself instructs us through the biblical texts.

Now plainly there is nothing new about this approach to marriage. Many writers have understood what is needed and have gone a long way to meet the need in both academic and more popular works. Nevertheless, the demand for a theological treatment has hardly been so fully met as to rule out another look more directly at God himself and marriage. Nor have all Christians — even those who have studied the biblical data — considered this more personal aspect of their marriages or weighed all its implications for their attitudes and conduct in them.

In itself a book on the theology of marriage will not solve every modern marital problem. Nor will it necessarily arrest the serious decline in the solidity of Christian marriage. It will, however, present what is for many people a new dimension by stressing the outlook and activity of God himself in the situation. It will offer the chance of a new appraisal and a new approach in the light of God's own participation. It will divert attention from pressing but often comparatively petty difficulties to the broader scope and purpose and nature of marriage and the resultant privileges and responsibilities of Christian partners in it. By presenting these aspects, it will pose the practical question: What manner of marriage ought we to have if these things are so? It will then pose the secondary question: What manner of marriage do we actually have by comparison or contrast?

In other words, a theology of marriage can give a new direction. Far too many people, Christians not excluded, are self-centeredly preoccupied with their own marital problems and their attempt to engineer solutions to them. A theology of marriage can help them to achieve a God-centered look at the larger situation of which their marriages constitute a small, if by no means unimportant, part. In the long run a new look means a new understanding, and a new understanding means a new practice. Another book on marriage needs no further justification.

I

God the Creator and Marriage

1. THE CREATION

Marriage goes back to God's beginning with the human race. This cannot be said of all institutions. State, society, law, economy, and politics all came later. Even family has to be called secondary to marriage. With marriage we go back, if not of course to God's own beginning, at any rate to humanity's beginning with God. In different ways, both of the creation stories in Genesis make this point.

According to the first story, in Genesis 1, God made man (generic) in his own image. In parallelism or parenthesis, or perhaps both, the verse adds: "Male and female created he them" (1:27). As has often been pointed out, this is not a direct reference to marriage. God did not create man husband and wife. What he created was the sexual distinction in unity (man as male and female) which forms the larger background of marriage.

In some way that is not defined, this creation of man as male and female seems to stand in relation to creation in God's image, which is also not defined. Possibly the existence of two distinct beings, man and woman, who are both generically man, reflects in a loose way God's own being as three persons, Father, Son, and Holy Spirit, who are all equally God. If so, Paul's argument in 1

1

Corinthians 11:1-12 takes on a deeper significance. But whatever the connection, God obviously planned and created human life as life within this distinction in unity, and by associating it with his own being, he conferred on it a high ranking and dignity.

Whether within marriage or outside of it, this distinction in unity forms an integral and inescapable part of human reality. It denotes the broader relation of the sexes in which no male can exist without the female and no female without the male. When humanity multiplies, people may live single lives or even lives segregated according to sex. They may avoid both marriage and sex itself in the narrow sense. Yet they cannot get outside the common structure of human life. Single men will have, or will have had, at least, a mother, and single women a father, along with the necessary grandmothers and grandfathers whom they might well have known in their early years. It is also highly probable that they will have, or will have had, sisters, brothers, aunts, uncles, nieces, nephews, cousins, and, for a period at least, some friends or acquaintances of the opposite sex. God has made sexuality in this wider sense an essential element in being human. No one can escape it.

Already in Genesis 1, however, this broader relation takes on a narrower focus. God has a purpose for man as man and woman. The commission is given that they should have dominion over the rest of creation. God appoints them his stewards. (Possibly this office also has to do with their being in the divine image.) He appoints both of them his stewards: "God said to *them*. . ." (1:28). He does not give the male the right of government apart from the female nor does he give to either of them the right of ownership, exploitation, or absolute and autonomous rule. As stewards of God, they are to be conservators and trustees. Bound up with this commission is a prior command that they should be fruitful and multiply, not merely as an end in itself, but in order that the stewardship of God's bountiful creation might be possible. Propagation of the race demands that man and woman come together in the special union of male and female which makes procreation possible and which distinguishes marriage from every other relationship of the sexes. In creating man as male and female God not only creates sexuality in the broad sense as integral to created humanity; he also institutes marriage as a specific expression and fulfilment of the sexual relation. In this first story, by inference from the divine commission, marriage itself goes back to God's beginning with us and ours with God. Incidentally, it also carries with it the beginning of the family and the continuing possibility of marriage, so that both marriage first and family second have their origin, basis, and goal in the divine purpose, word, and action.

The second creation story, in Genesis 2, looks at things from a different angle. Here God makes the male first. He notes, however, the inadequacy of the solitary life (2:18). He brings the animals to Adam as possible companions ("helpmeets"). They offer relationship of a kind but not authentic fellowship because they lack the necessary ingredient of equality (2:19f.). God then provides the new and true companion who can be this because, being taken out of man, she is distinct yet no less authentically and equally human ("bone of my bones and flesh of my flesh," 2:23). The coming together of man and woman — their marriage — constitutes a unity ("they become one flesh," 2:24) which carries with it the fulness of fellowship — companionship is emphasized here — and the perfecting of humanity itself.

God is the author of this union. It corresponds to his will for the race. Relationship with all creation is included but at its deepest level relationship means the closest possible fellowship of one human being with another being who is equally human yet also different. The male has a certain priority in this relation, for the woman is taken from the man and not the other way round. Yet priority is not the point of the story. The equal humanity which is needed for full companionship takes precedence. As in the Trinity the Father, as the fount of deity, has a certain precedence over the Son and the Spirit, yet all are equally God in eternal interrelation, so it is with man and woman in the fellowship which God has purposed and created.

Can we really call this union marriage? If so, what are its characteristic features? The final verses in Genesis 2 (24f.) provide clear answers to both questions. Leaving father and mother for the sake of a woman carries an obvious reference to marriage; indeed, verse 24 speaks of a man cleaving to his wife. Whether or not there is a related ceremonial or institutional form is immaterial here. Furthermore, the verses tell us three elementary and fundamental things about marriage. First, it is the most important relationship, for which even family ties will in a sense be broken. This break does not come easily, especially in the circumstances of human life subsequent to the fall. Yet, for the sake of marriage "a man leaves his father and his mother." Children, too, will always have to come within the context of the primary relation. Second, marriage is designed to be a lasting union. This is indicated by the words "cleave to" and even more so by the fact that husband and wife "become one flesh," entering into a deep and unbreakable unity (v. 24). Third, it involves an intimacy of fellowship even at the most basic physical level; they are naked to one another without shame (v. 25). In marriage God has given us the basis and climax of all human fellowship from which all other forms derive and in which they find their primary model.

It has often been pointed out that in Genesis 2:24 the union of man and woman in marriage is complete in itself without children. The commission of 1:28 stands, yet marriage has its own perfection without having to be related to family. It will retain this perfection when it is accompanied by the family relation and also after children have left to pursue their own adult ways. A fruitful suggestion is that the glorification of sexual love in the Song of Songs celebrates this perfection, the frankness of statement being offensive or embarrassing only to those who suffer the inhibiting effects of the fall. Be that as it may, the provision of a fit helpmeet completes in itself the circle of fellowship in humanity.

The primacy of the Creator God in the whole process that is set before us in the two stories should be emphasized again in conclusion. God willed to create man in his image, male and female, and he did so. God gave male and female the commission to replenish the earth and subdue it, so that reproduction has a theological and not just a biological and sociological validation. God made man of the dust of the earth, established a relation between man and animals, and then made of man a similar but different being who could be an adequate helpmeet. As God authored humanity in general, so he authored the primal relation within it which comes to its fullest expression in marriage. Marriage lies within the gracious purpose of God for the race and its constitution comes directly with his creative word and work.

2. THE FALL

The divine basis and context of marriage explains why obedience to the will of God is so important for it. Marriage can work only as it conforms to the purpose and work of him who created and established it. In this it resembles all other relationships, whether with other human beings or with the larger world of nature and animals. Inner human harmony depends on harmony with God. Conversely, disruption of harmony with God means disruption of inner human harmony. This disruption will be felt most keenly at the closest and therefore the most sensitive point of relationship. Marriage stands to lose most if disobedience interferes with the relation to God and hampers the fulfilment of his plan for the creature.

Disobedience is possible because God did not create automatons but beings with their own powers of thought and will. (Is this another meaning of being made in God's image?) Disobedience is not just possible but real, for according to the story in Genesis 3, the man and woman foolishly and gullibly and arrogantly reject the way of the Creator, choose a way of their own that they believe to be better, and in so doing spoil their relation not only with God but also with one another and with the world in which they have been set.

The act of disobedience has no specific connection with marriage. Yet indirectly it involves marriage and directly it has a disastrous impact upon it. It involves marriage indirectly because the woman makes a unilateral decision when she eats the fruit. She does not pause to consult her husband in mutuality of choice and actions. Similarly, the man tamely submits to his partner's judgment ("she also gave some to her husband, and he ate," v.6) without weighing the matter independently. He thus restores a false mutuality in wrongdoing. On a strict view of the priority of the male, one might even say that a reversal of positions takes place in the whole event and that this is itself a part of the initial disorder. Whether this be true or not, the neglect of mutuality and its restoration on a false basis undoubtedly belong to the sin. Marriage suffers disorder already in the disobedient act.

The direct impact of disobedience may be seen at once in a series of rapid consequences. First, the man and woman, knowing good

5

and evil, come under the sway of a guilty self-consciousness. As the Bible tersely puts it, "they knew that they were naked" (v. 7). Shame enters the beautiful relation of 2:25 and spoils it. They try to counter this new factor by making concealing garments but the perfection of marriage as God planned and created it has suffered serious loss.

Second, a distortion of the partnership itself occurs. This takes the form of male supremacy and rule. God himself states the new situation: Woman's desire shall be for her husband and the husband shall rule over her (3:16). The mutuality of marriage, injured already in the act of the fall, gives place to a hierarchy which contains the seeds of brutality, resentment, rivalry, and conflict. If marriage itself remains, its proper realization becomes infinitely more difficult.

Third, man is estranged from nature. Both male and female forfeit the harmonious environment which God had willed and made for them. They now have to live out their partnership not only with its own inner distortion but also in the damaging circumstances of exacting toil and material care. The burden this time falls heavily on the male: "Cursed is the ground because of you. . . . in the sweat of your face you shall eat bread" (3:17ff.). But the woman obviously must share the labor and anxiety and suffer equally from the tensions which these entail.

The central problem of the fall is not the relationship of marriage but the relationship to God. Man and woman think they know better than God and defy him instead of obeying him. In so doing, they bring down disaster upon themselves. God does not need to impose special penalties. The consequences themselves are penalties. They become divine judgments, as the curses of 3:15ff. make clear. Yet in pronouncing these judgments, God is not accepting the man-made situation in place of his own original design. He lets the man and woman see where their disobedience leads, not least in terms of their own disturbed relation to one another. But he does not acquiesce in this as a new and final state. He still retains his own purpose. Even before he shows how those who did not want what he planned will be affected by their refusal, he announces a work of deliverance and restoration.

He does this in veiled form in the promise of 3:15. The descendant of the woman, though suffering lesser injury from the serpent, will bruise its head. God through the human race will snatch back the victory from his opponents, if not without cost. The relationship to God himself will be restored. With it will come the restoration of human relationships too. No second best, no interim measure, no situation dictated by opposition, will finally be allowed for marriage. Even as the results of disobedience come upon it as judgments, God intimates and initiates the work of rescue and restitution.

3. THE FALLEN CREATURE

The Bible is a painfully honest and realistic book. It does not invent unbelievably good people nor tell stories with necessarily happy endings. It does not omit even some of the more sordid details of human character and conduct. It portrays people and situations as they are, attractive, or repulsive, or a mixture of both.

This characteristic of holy scripture strikes the reader at once when the period after the fall is studied. This epoch bears eloquent testimony to the complete disintegration of human relationships which results from the break in the relationship with God. As Paul indicates in Romans (1:18ff.), God does not intervene directly to halt this process. Rather, he imposes the restraining judgments of the flood and the tower of Babel. He also makes the so-called covenant with Noah to sanction certain safeguards of retributive justice. Yet in the main he lets the race live with the consequences of its own folly, giving it up to the dishonoring of the body, to dishonorable passions, to a base mind and improper conduct (Rom. 1:24, 26, 28). Thus, the march of violence and corruption continues across the centuries with all the toll of human wretchedness and suffering that it exacts.

The primary relationship of marriage enjoys no exemption from the general rule. Already in Genesis 4:19, the two who are one flesh have become three as the masterful Lamech takes two wives. To these wives he boasts of a bloody deed of vengeance (4:23f.) in a typical blending of violence and sexual immoderation. Genesis 6 records what seems to be a further deterioration whose precise form constitutes an enigma: "The sons of God came in to the daughters of men, and they bore children to them" (6:4).

7

It is in the context of this happening that God says, "My spirit shall not abide in man for ever," and provides a further safeguard by shortening the span of human life (6:3).

In spite of the judgments of the flood and the tower of Babel, the age of the patriarchs, which is in no way idealized, brings no substantial change. The patriarchs themselves, with whom God commences his specific work of salvation, are guilty of many of the sexual irregularities which characterize their times. Abram in self-protection makes a shabby arrangement with Sarai his wife which allows her to become part of Pharaoh's harem (Gen. 12:11ff.; cf. 20:1ff.). Not trusting God that he will give them the promised child in spite of their advancing age, Abram and Sarai try to take the initiative by agreeing that Sarai's maid Hagar shall serve as a second wife (Gen. 16:1ff.). And even though God blesses Hagar in spite of the tangled situation (Gen. 16:7ff.; 21:15ff.), this does not avert the evils that follow: the rift between Abram and Sarai, the jealousy and cruelty of Sarai, the original triumphant scorn of Hagar, the quarrel about the children, and finally the expulsion of Hagar and Ishmael. Hardly the pattern of a happy and successful marriage!

Isaac and Rebekah seem to avoid the marital problems of the previous generation. Through their children, however, tensions develop which obviously strain the original relationship. Life is made bitter for both of them by the marriages of Esau with the Hittite women Judith and Basemath (Gen. 26:34; 27:46; 36:2ff.). Furthermore, Rebekah's favoring of Jacob, the younger twin, leads to the deceiving of Isaac, the cheating of Esau, a distortion of the marital relation, and a quarrel in the family which will not be resolved until Jacob returns from enforced exile many years later (Gen. 27:14ff.; 32:2ff.; 33).

The marriages of Esau and Jacob both involve problems that are no less severe than those faced by many people today. Esau not only takes two wives but he takes them from outside the patriarchal family and its commitment to God. Jacob undergoes the ironic experience of being himself deceived and finding himself with an unwanted wife, Leah (Gen. 29:21ff.). When he adds Rachel as his second and preferred wife (29:28ff.), jealousy erupts, and in the competition to provide Jacob with children the maids Bilhah and Zilpah are enlisted as auxiliary wives, adding to the confusion of Jacob's married life (Gen. 30:1ff.). Later we read that Reuben, the eldest son, had an illicit relation to the concubine Bilhah (Gen. 35:22); when his father heard about this it led to his exclusion from a position of preeminence among the twelve sons (Gen. 49:4). In spite of his love for Rachel, Jacob's whole marital experience is a far cry from the "one flesh" which was the original purpose and institution of God the Creator.

The records give evidence of decline rather than improvement as the patriarchal history continues. The episode of Shechem and Dinah, the daughter of Jacob, begins with the violence of rape and ends with revenge, treachery, and the even greater violence of murder (Gen. 34). The dealings of Judah and his sons with Tamar represent a sorry mixture of injustice, intrigue, and sensuality (Gen. 38). The inherited jealousies in Jacob's own family work themselves out in the plot against Joseph and the callous deception of Jacob regarding the fate of his favorite son. Not only does Judah marry a Canaanite (Shua) with sorry results, but even Joseph marries the Egyptian Asenath, daughter of Potiphera, the priest of On (Gen. 41:45).

The lesson of the whole period subsequent to the fall is plain. In a world of developing disobedience, marriage becomes a problem instead of a promise. The fall from God lies behind all the failure and misery in what God designed to be so fulfilling a relationship. The biblical stories strip away any illusions that one might entertain in this regard, especially under the influence of romantic dreams of marrying in ecstacy and living happily ever after. (New tensions in marriage today are simply old tensions in new forms.) At this early stage, before God's work of redemption and restoration has been carried through, even members of the chosen patriarchal family fall victim to the same chaos and confusion as all the rest.

Yet God does not allow marriage to perish totally, nor its true form to be totally obscured. In the dark conditions of the patriarchal age some brighter features may be discerned which carry promise for the future. First, a bond of true love exists between many of the husbands and wives. This seems often to be implied, though not explicitly stated, in the tangled story of Abraham and Sarah. It finds explicit statement in the case of Isaac and Rebekah. The arrangement of this marriage by Abraham's servant Eliezer

(Gen. 24) might seem to hold out no great hope for a deep marital love. But the story takes a surprising turn. Meditating in the field by evening, Isaac sees the camels coming, brings Rebekah to his tent, takes her as his wife, and, as the record tells us in the simplest possible terms: "He loved her." A similar love, distinguished for its faithfulness across many years of trial and disappointment, ‧arises in the case of Jacob and Rachel. Jacob loves Rachel, probably from their first meeting at the well (Gen. 29:9ff., 18), and so great is this love that the seven years of service "seemed to him but a few days" because of it (29:20) and he was willing to serve another seven years in return for marrying her (Gen. 29:27ff.). Even in the grim story of Shechem and Dinah it is worth noting that Shechem, although he commits the fatal sin of raping Dinah, is said to have loved her so much that he, too, was ready to meet any condition if only she might be given to him as his wife (Gen. 34:12).

Second, a conspicuous feature of the complicated marriages of the period is their enduring character. Through all the difficulties, one of the only instances of a break of any kind is when Sarah enforces the dismissal of Hagar. Trouble arises between Rebekah and Isaac when Rebekah brings about the replacement of Esau by Jacob in regard to the birthright, but the marriage itself continues. We also read that Jacob "loved Rachel more than Leah" (Gen. 29:30), and even that "Leah was hated" (29:31); yet, in spite of the fact that Leah had been foisted upon him by a trick, Jacob never thought of ending the marriage. In most of the marriages, especially when polygamy or concubinage occurred, almost intolerable strains were put on the relationships. Nevertheless, whether due to conviction, convention, convenience, family considerations, or social and economic conditions, the marriages held together and the partners worked their way as best they could through the difficulties, perhaps recognizing that all human relationships involve problems in the world as it now is.

A final and partially related point is that the patriarchs prefer marriages within the family. Abraham, for example, refuses to let Isaac find a wife among the Canaanites (Gen. 24:3). Isaac, tired of the wives of Esau, takes the same position in relation to Jacob (Gen. 28:1), not without some prompting from Rebekah (27:46).

Even Esau, when he sees that his Canaanite wives do not please his father, takes another wife from the family of Ishmael (28:8f.). Others, it is true, marry outside the family: Judah marries the Canaanite Shua and Joseph the Egyptian Asenath, though Joseph takes care to have his sons Ephraim and Manasseh blessed by his father Jacob (Gen. 48). On the human side the desire for marital separateness testifies to the common wish to avoid intermingling with other groups, peoples, or races, but within the divinely selected patriarchal family it takes on a deeper and better founded theological significance which emerges from the continuing story of Israel.

Where does God appear in this record of patriarchal marriages? He appears first in judgment. To be sure, we find only isolated interventions in the form of specific judgments (Gen. 38:7, 10). Once again God's judgment is to let the desires and deeds of men and women run their course and be their own punishment. Distortions of marriage abound and they carry with them the evil consequences that the Bible so honestly and graphically depicts. They cause both mental and physical pain and suffering in what ought to be the happiest of relationships. As Jacob puts it, somewhat rhetorically yet not wholly unrealistically, to Pharaoh: "Few and evil have been the days of the years of my life" (Gen. 47:9). God had no need to impose particular penalties. As marriages still illustrate today, the marital disorder introduced by sin imposes penalty enough of its own.

God also appears in grace. This takes a new form in the patriarchal age. God has begun to work out the promises of redemption and reconstruction. After all, the interesting aspect of the records of the period is not that they offer more and more examples of sin and judgment. Behind the whole story of Abraham and Sarah and their family stands the divine call and covenant. God will use this family, with all its faults and fallibilities, as the means whereby salvation will come to the race. His grace may be seen in his guidance of the patriarchs, in his provision for them, in his preservation of them, and in his forbearance with and forgiveness of them. It may be seen in both the crises and the everyday events. It may be seen not least of all in the marriages, for it is through marriage and the family that salvation will finally come in the personal form of the Savior, who is their descendant.

The divine action in the patriarchal marriages finds clearest expression in the detailed story of the arrangement of Isaac's marriage in Genesis 24. Abraham lays the whole matter in the hands of God (24:7). His servant prays for clear leading when he reaches the well at evening (12ff.). He waits for the verdict of God (v. 21) and gives thanks to God for it (v. 27). In answer to his testimony Laban and Bethuel have to admit that "the thing comes from the Lord" (v. 50). The special love of Isaac for a bride whom he has not previously seen seems to seal the divine leading, as something of the original purpose of the Creator in marriage is recaptured. The lesson of the story is not just the moral one that believers should pray for God's guidance in their own marriages, good though this is. What counts is that Abraham and his servant are right. God does in fact overrule here as in all the decisive dealings with Abraham. As marriage comes from God in creation, so it serves God in salvation.

The active role of God in patriarchal marriage sheds a new light, as we have suggested, on marriage within the family. As Abraham understands it, this is not just a matter of ordinary aloofness from strange peoples. God himself wills it. He has chosen this family as his own family within which he will work out his revealing and reconciling purpose. Here, then, is a special family. Its separateness is "holiness," the separateness of the people of God's gracious election. Thus, the aggravation of foreign wives goes beyond that of purely human difference. Even if only dimly recognized, it has a theological aspect. The separateness, of course, is ultimately that of service, not superiority. It is a real separateness which will characterize God's people in every age. In spite of its apparent harshness, it has its basis in grace. It takes this form in order that salvation might come to all peoples. It does so in order that within the people of God's salvation a measure of authentic marriage and authentic marital love, which will be a witness to God's renewing work in the world, may be attained again.

A final point should not be missed. In and through the failings and follies of the patriarchs in their marriages, God maintains sovereign control in the accomplishment of his own purpose. He will not allow Abram and Sarai to solve the problem of promised succession on their own, but against all expectation gives them the child of his own choosing, namely, Isaac. When Jacob prefers

Rachel to Leah, this does not alter the fact that God's line will go through Judah, the child of Leah, not through Joseph, the child of Rachel, even though Joseph is the favorite son and the one through whom God works out his immediate purposes for Israel. God does not tie his own hands here. If he overrules human plans and choices, he also overrules human ideas of legitimacy and succession. The election of Jacob and the dispossession of Reuben make this plain. God does not condone, let alone sponsor, wrongdoing. Yet his saving grace is sovereign grace. He wills that his will be done, and in spite of human deviation and opposition, he takes care that it is done. He does this in order that the race which refused to do it, and now for the most part does it only unwillingly and unwittingly, may finally do it voluntarily and joyfully and spontaneously as the work of restoration comes to completion.

II

The God of Israel and Marriage

1. THE LAW OF ISRAEL

God's history with the human race, and specifically with the patri-archal family, takes a decisive turn at the exodus from Egypt. The enslaved descendants of Jacob and his sons now become an eman-cipated people, make their way slowly to the land of promise, and gradually establish a national life, first very loosely under the judges, then more cohesively under the single monarchy, and at last dividedly in the separate kingdoms. In this dramatically changed and changing situation God as the God of Israel does and says some new and decisive things both in the life of the people as a whole and particularly in relation to marriage as a distinctive and significant sphere within it.

The giving of the law for the direction and protection of the liberated people constitutes perhaps the most important of all the new developments. This divine legislation takes two forms: first, the fundamental or principial form of the decalogue, and second, the applied and detailed form of specific laws and punishments. The first might be described more generally as the moral law, the second as civil and criminal law. This obviously does not imply that the two forms are antithetical. They are in fact complemen-tary.

As the record in Exodus tells us, Israel receives the moral law both verbally (Exod. 20) and then on tablets of stone which Moses brings down from his meeting with God on Mt. Sinai (Exod. 25ff.). Of the ten commandments thus given, two relate specifically to marriage. The seventh (Exod. 20:14) issues a strict prohibition of adultery, the act whereby a married partner has sex relations either outside marriage or within another marriage, and is thus unfaithful to, or a violator of, the unity that marriage entails. The tenth (Exod. 20:17) digs more deeply and rules out any coveting of the spouse of another, the desire which may precede the adulterous act or may indeed exist independently of it. Neither in desire nor act is Israel to injure or destroy the married partnership. Instead, it is to respect and uphold it as the fundamental relationship which God established with his creation of man as both male and female.

The detailed legislation offers more direct guidance and protection for marriage in the form of specific enactments and penalties. These may be found for the most part in three rounds of lawgiving in Exodus 21ff., Leviticus 19f., and Deuteronomy 21ff. The laws deal with particular problems, some more directly related to the historical setting, others of more general range and relevance. Not all have equal importance but none can be dismissed as trivial or valueless.

The legislation in Exodus first provides safeguards for the female slave whose master designates her for himself or his son but then either rejects her or takes another wife. She must either receive food, clothes, and marital rights, or else she must be granted her freedom (21:7ff.). Similarly, an unbetrothed woman who is seduced cannot be abandoned. An offer of marriage must be made, and if her father will not sanction the marriage, a money payment has to be made instead (22:16f.). Both enactments check male irresponsibility.

The group in Leviticus exempts from the general penalty for fornication a master and his female slave who have intercourse even though the slave is already engaged to someone else (19:20); instead, it specifies that the owner must make a guilt offering in atonement. It includes a strong law (although with no designated penalty) against giving up a daughter to prostitution (20:29). The offence of adultery carries a death sentence for both guilty parties, as does incest (20:10ff.). A list of prohibitions of marriages with close relatives is given in the Leviticus code (18:6ff.). Intercourse with such relatives, along with relationships with the same sex or with animals, carries with it both the specific penalty of banishment from the people and a general threat of eviction of the whole people from the land (18:24ff.). Some special provisions for priests should be noted. To uphold the sanctity of the hereditary priesthood they are not to marry widows, divorcees, prostitutes, or any women who have been defiled, but only virgins (21:14f.).

Outside the main group in Deuteronomy an isolated rule in chapter 7 (vv. 3f.) sternly forbids intermarrying with the previous inhabitants of Canaan. The restriction cites the danger of seduction into idolatry as the reason. In the main Deuteronomic legislation an important law protects the rights of the firstborn in a polygamous marriage (polygamy is nowhere forbidden) even when he is the son of a wife who is disliked (21:15ff.). Wives also receive protection from husbands who falsely accuse them of shameful conduct and threaten to destroy their reputation (22:13ff.). The law against rape covers three different situations (22:23ff.). If a betrothed woman is raped, and she has the chance to cry for help but does not take it, both she and the rapist are to be stoned. If, however, she has no chance to seek help, the rapist alone is to be put to death. If the woman is not betrothed, the same rule applies as in Exodus 22:16f.: the rapist must marry her, the only difference being that no mention is now made of objection on the part of the woman's father. As in Leviticus, both a man and a woman who are guilty of adultery come under a capital sentence (22:22).

Deuteronomy contains an interesting and important rule on divorce, which the first two groups do not discuss. Only the husband seems to have the right of divorce. Finding some "indecency" in the wife constitutes the rather ambivalent ground. He has to give his wife a bill of divorce. She, like the husband, may marry again. If, however, the second husband dies or divorces her, reconstitution of the first marriage is forbidden (24:1-4).

In spite of the prohibition of marriages with close relatives, Deuteronomy allows and even commands Levirate marriage. If a man dies without children, his brother (or nearest male relative) must marry the widow in order to perpetuate the name of the deceased husband (25:5ff.). Refusal to discharge this obligation brings down moral obloquy.

Besides the legislation, Deuteronomy also contains a number of curses which the Levites declare with a loud voice and the people accepts by saying "Amen." Among the accursed are those who commit various forms of incest (27:11ff., especially 20 and 22f.).

At various periods in Christian history, the church and even the state have adopted some of these laws for their own members. In general, however, expositors agree that, as specific enactments with attached penalties, they apply strictly and properly only to the Old Testament period when God's people is also a nation with its own legal and social institutions. In this regard, the detailed rules differ from the ten commandments. The commandments do not deal with individual situations or prescribe penalties (apart from the general judgment of God). They have a more general moral character and describe the conduct which God wills or does not will for the human creature. Adultery, as a breach of the basic relationship of marriage, holds a place among the things that fall outside the divine will and purpose. So does the coveting of the wives of others which underlies the adulterous act.

What purpose does the law serve within the divine plan? Three functions may be mentioned. All of them apply to the law of marriage in particular as well as to the law in general.

First, God uses the law to guide his liberated people in the new life which she will lead as the people of God in the land of God's promise. While in bondage in Egypt, Israel had come under the legislation of a foreign power. She now has the opportunity to develop her own mode of life and conduct. As the people of God, she should adopt a way that is also God's way. In marriage as in other matters, certain things are proper for her and other things are to be avoided. The law shows both in general and in detail how she may shape her life in conformity to God's will for her.

In contrast to the injunctions of the New Testament, these directions are for a people whose deliverance is more temporal than spiritual. They do not come, then, with a spiritual power of fulfilment. They relate more to the externalities of actions than their inner motivations and compulsions. They take the form of definite laws and in most cases carry civil penalties to enforce compliance. They prefigure the work of salvation but do not yet fulfil it.

Second, God uses the law to protect the life of the people from disintegration through self-interest, force, and violence. As one will have noted, most of the detailed laws take a negative, not a positive form. They provide safeguards for marriage and for the parties involved, especially the weaker parties. They cannot deal with every possible disorder, though. They leave the field open for many evils such as those associated with polygamy. Yet they go some way toward fixing and stabilizing the marital relation and protecting married people from the worst distortions that can so easily result from human sinfulness.

Many theologians have seen this to be a continuing function of the law — or of law in general — which Christians should endorse. Even if the particular rules of the Old Testament need not (all) be adopted, social stability demands legislation for marriage — preferably the best legislation — as a matter of public concern. Hence, Christians must ask themselves whether as citizens they should not work to establish the best laws for the safeguarding of marriage. Even if they neither can nor should try to legislate the Christian view and practice of marriage, does not law still have a protective function and should they not join with others who have a concern for social cohesion in seeking legislation that will best accomplish this end? Or are Christians committed exclusively to a more specific and distinctive mission?

Third, the law serves a teleological purpose in relation to the gospel which emerges fully only with the New Testament. It exposes the human situation by promulgating commandments and laying down regulations which Israel is in fact unable to keep. The moral law fulfils this function on a broad scale; the detailed laws fulfil it more specifically. In spite of the seventh and tenth commandments, adultery and the coveting of others' spouses do not cease. Many people in Israel and many more across the centuries and continents fall short in relation to one or another of the detailed laws or other marital disorders which are left unspecified. An indictment is thus pronounced against the human distortion of marriage in comparison with and contrast to what God himself requires. As Paul puts it so forcefully in Romans, this indictment convicts us of both our guilt and our inability to be anything but guilty. To find forgiveness and renewal it is not enough to make more strenuous efforts to keep the law. We must look and turn to the pardon which God provides through the reconciling work of Jesus Christ and the renewal which he effects through the regenerating ministry of the Holy Spirit.

2. THE PRACTICE OF ISRAEL

Illustrations of the failure of Israel to keep the commandments and the laws of marriage may be found in plenty as the nation moves across the desert, settles in the land under the judges, establishes herself with the monarchy, and then goes into exile and returns. We must remember, of course, that at all periods many people did in fact avoid the act of adultery and kept to the letter of the marriage code. Even though the law convicts us of sin and need, not all are guilty of breaking the law at all points. The situation changes, of course, when it comes to the thoughts and intents of the heart.

Collectively, the weakness of Israel emerges already during the desert journey. Coming near to the land of promise the people lodges for a time at Shittim. Here, we read, "the people began to play the harlot with the daughters of Moab" (Num. 25:1). These sexual irregularities committed with members of foreign nations lead quickly to idolatry as well. The daughters of Moab "invited the people to the sacrifices of their gods, and the people ate, and bowed down to their gods" (25:2). Thus "Israel yoked himself to Baal of Peor" (25:3). Even when judgment falls on the people because of this offence, a certain Zimri, son of a head of a father's house, brings a Midianitess, Cozbi, openly to his dwelling (25:6ff.), where they are both put to death by Phinehas, Aaron's grandson (Num. 25; see also Deut. 4:3; Ps. 106:28ff.).

The anarchical period of the judges produces one of the most astonishing and disheartening of all episodes. It begins with a separation. The concubine of a Levite from Ephraim becomes angry with him and returns to her home in Bethlehem. The Levite goes after her and persuades her to come back with him. On the way, however, they are assaulted while staying with an old man in Sibeah and the woman is handed over to the assailants to try to pacify them. They rape and kill her. In reply, the other tribes attack and almost annihilate the guilty tribe of Benjamin, leaving only six hundred men alive. Then, in order that the tribe not be utterly blotted out, four hundred girls are taken from the non-cooperative city of Jabesh-gilead and given to the Benjaminites. To make up the deficit, the latter are also allowed to seize the young women of Shiloh who come out to the dances at the annual feast of the Lord (Judges 19-21). As the author wryly and real-istically comments when he brings the story and the whole book to a conclusion: "In those days. . .every man did what was right in his own eyes" (21:25).

Even at a much later time, after the establishment and over-throw of the monarchy and the chastening experience of the exile, a mass movement toward mixed marriages takes place. Both Ezra and Nehemiah have to deal with this in their efforts to reconstruct the community and put it on a more solid material, moral, and spiritual footing. In Ezra 10 Shecaniah confesses on behalf of the community: "We have broken faith with our God and have mar-ried foreign women from the people of the land" (10:2). The in-vestigation of the matter takes several weeks and the list of priests and Levites among those who are affected testifies to the extent of the infraction. The problem is present under Nehemiah too, who takes vigorous physical measures against the offenders when he finds that some of their children cannot even speak their own language: "I. . .beat some of them and pulled out their hair; and I made them take oath in the name of God, saying, 'You shall not give your daughters to their sons, or take their daughters for your sons or for yourselves' " (Neh. 13:23ff.). Probably to the same period, or a little before, belongs the charge of Malachi that some of the people are abandoning the wives of their youth and the covenant so as to marry the daughters of strange gods. This leads to a very strong statement against divorce which takes on a general character, even though it is uttered in the specific context of separation for the sake of remarriage outside of Israel: "I hate divorce, says the Lord the God of Israel. . . . So take heed to your-selves and do not be faithless" (Mal. 2:16).

Individually, marital irregularities seem to fall into three main categories: those associated with adultery and polygamy, those as-sociated with foreign marriages, and those associated with idola-try. These three are often interrelated, even to the point of overlapping, as the various episodes illustrate.

The most famous instance of adultery is obviously that of David and Bathsheba. It begins with the glance which leads to the covetous desire which is forbidden by the last commandment (2 Sam. 11:2ff.). Having royal power at his command, David rapidly translates the desire into the act, thereby breaking the seventh commandment as well (11:4). When a child is conceived, the evil of adultery involves David in the further sins of deceit (a cover-up) and the treacherous murder of his loyal officer Uriah (11:6ff.). Belated marriage with Bathsheba after the death of her husband (11:27) simply opens the door to the further troubles which result from wholesale polygamy on the part of the king.

Next to the transgression of David perhaps the most glaring offence is that of his son Amnon (2 Sam. 13). Amnon comes to love his beautiful half-sister Tamar, the full sister of Absalom. Having no way of approaching her, he pretends to be ill, and when his father visits him, he asks that Tamar might prepare and serve a meal for him. The stratagem succeeds, but when Tamar resists Amnon's advances, he takes her by force in spite of her plea that if they wait perhaps the king will arrange their marriage. Having done his will, Amnon promptly comes to hate Tamar: "The hatred with which he hated her was greater than the love with which he had loved her" (2 Sam. 13:15). He puts her out roughly, even though she pleads that doing so is a greater wrong to her than the rape itself. The evil results of the incident are part of the more general problem of polygamy and may be noted briefly in that context.

As already noted, polygamy is permitted under the law. Hence it is no direct offence to engage in it. Nevertheless, even on a small scale, it can still bring almost intolerable tensions into marriage and cause a great deal of suffering. The story of Hannah (1 Sam. 1f.) offers a familiar example. Hannah is one of the two wives of Elkanah. She is greatly loved by her husband but has no children. Peninnah, the other wife, has both sons and daughters and uses this advantage to provoke and humiliate Hannah. This must have been a common situation, and even where there were children by both wives, jealousies and rivalries added to the general strains on the relationship of marriage and family.

Practiced on a bigger scale, as by the kings of Israel who

imitated foreign rulers in this regard, polygamy could raise a whole set of serious problems. Ultimately, the most serious was that of potential (and actual) turning away from God. As Deuteronomy says with respect to the king: "He shall not multiply wives for himself, lest his heart turn away" (17:17). Wholesale polygamy falls outside the limits of what is permissible in marriage. If it does so primarily because of the danger of apostasy or idolatry, as will be seen later, it also brings its own virulent poison into the family life of the polygamist.

The story of Amnon and Tamar might be viewed from this angle both in its substance and in its consequences. In substance the presence of many half-brothers and half-sisters in fairly close proximity presents temptations which explain even if they do not excuse the conduct of Amnon. Yet when Amnon takes the course he does, it brings irreparable discord into the family. Absalom, when he hears what has been done to his sister, plots deadly revenge. He, too, uses the pretext of a meal. He invites Amnon with all the king's sons to a sheepshearing banquet, presses the invitation against David's objections, and then has his half-brother murdered at the feast. Nor does the story end there, for after his exile and return, Absalom almost succeeds in ousting his father, publicly sporting with his concubines when he occupies Jerusalem (2 Sam. 16ff.). The full consequences come home to David personally when his forces achieve victory at the cost of the life of his much loved son: "Would that I had died instead of you, O Absalom, my son, my son!" (2 Sam. 18:33).

The situation becomes even more tragic with David's last illness. Adonijah, the son of Haggith, and Solomon, the son of Bathsheba, are the chief contenders for the throne, each with powerful support in both church and state. Even before David's death, Adonijah tries to take control, but Bathsheba and Nathan the prophet gain the support of the dying David for the anointing and proclamation of Solomon as king. Once Solomon is firmly set on the throne, he eliminates Adonijah and even arranges the death of the old army commander Joab, son of Zeruaiah, David's sister (1 Kings 1-2). An even more bloody massacre takes place when Athaliah, mother of Ahaziah, decides to take over Judah on the death of her son. She destroys all the royal family apart from Joash, who is rescued by Ahaziah's sister Jehosheba and hidden in the temple until the time comes for the overthrow of Athaliah (2 Kings 11).

The evils of foreign marriages may be seen dramatically in many individual cases reported in scripture. Samson offers a first example. Although enmity exists between Israel and the Philistines, and his godly parents strongly advise him against it, Samson marries a Philistine woman from Timnah (Judges 14:1ff.). The marriage goes wrong from the start. The Philistines try to use Samson's wife against him, and when he goes back home, they give her to his best man (14:15ff., 20). Samson takes revenge by burning up their food supplies, but then the Philistines burn both his wife and her father (15:6). The unpredictable Samson is next found visiting a harlot in Gaza, where he is almost captured (16:1ff.). He finally falls in love with Delilah of Sorek, whom the Philistines employ to bring about his downfall (16:4ff.).

Solomon, for all his wisdom, becomes the classic example of one who carries polygamy and mixed marriages to an extreme bordering on the absurd. As 1 Kings 11:1ff. very simply puts it: "King Solomon loved many foreign women. . . . He had seven hundred wives. . .and three hundred concubines." He no doubt contracted many of these marriages for diplomatic reasons, especially the initial marriage with the daughter of Pharaoh (3:1ff.), which carried with it a profitable alliance. Yet the result of these marriages was that "when Solomon was old his wives turned away his heart after other gods" (11:4). The serious divine punishment for this would be the loss of the ten northern tribes and the division of the monarchy in the days of his son and successor Rehoboam (12). No less disastrous in its effects, however, was the official introduction of all kinds of alien cults into the country, e.g., the worship of Ashtoreth, Chemosh, and Molech (11:5ff.). The warnings in Proverbs 3:16ff., 5:18ff., and 7:6ff. against forsaking the wife of one's youth and being enticed by a strange woman have something of an ironic ring when considered against the background of the practice of Solomon; perhaps they can be regarded as a reflection of his experience.

The evils of idolatry, which are bound up inextricably with marriage outside the people of God and their faith and worship, constitute the third form of marital transgression. In this field Ahab offers an even more graphic illustration than Solomon, for while the foreign marriages of the latter led to a more or less peaceful coexistence of true religion and false, the marriage of Ahab produces a state of mortal conflict. Again a diplomatic intention — alliance with Sidon — lies behind the union of Ahab with Jezebel, the daughter of Ethbaal of Sidon. To please his alien bride, Ahab builds a temple to Baal in Samaria, and sets up an altar to Baal in it (1 Kings 16:31ff.). But Jezebel is not content merely to have her own place of worship. When Elijah comes forward to declare God's will and judgment, she sets out, with Ahab's connivance, to replace the worship of God completely by that of Baal (18:17ff.). She also persuades the king to try to overthrow the divine law of inheritance in Israel in favor of royal absolutism by arranging the murder of Naboth (21). Only the resolute opposition of Elijah and his comparatively few supporters puts a stop to this dangerous attempt to accomplish a total rejection of God and his law in favor of alien beliefs and concepts of government. So great is Jezebel's influence that scripture says about Ahab: "There was none who sold himself to do what was evil in the sight of the Lord like Ahab, whom Jezebel his wife incited" (21:25). His repentance (21:27ff.) and subsequent death (22) greatly weaken Jezebel's influence. Yet she remains defiant to the very last, taunting Jehu with head adorned and painted eyes until he has her attendants fling her through the window (2 Kings 9:30ff.).

Athaliah, the wife of Joram, who was a granddaughter of Omri, father of Ahab, seems to have desired to play something of the same role in Judah as Jezebel did in Israel. In the main, however, the kings of Judah avoided the foreign marriages which caused so much religious confusion in the north. Possibly the recollection of Solomon's fall due to alien wives played some part in this. Nehemiah certainly appeals to this outstanding example when the problem arises after the exile: "Did not Solomon king of Israel sin on account of such women? . . .He was beloved by his God. . . nevertheless foreign women made even him to sin" (Neh. 13:26). This does not mean that the south is exempt from idolatry, for under the evil influence of the north idolatry gains an entry when such kings as Ahaz, Manasseh, and Zedekiah promote and practice it. Nor does the possibility of idolatry through foreign marriages cease entirely in Judah. The experience of the post-exilic community demonstrates this very clearly. "The holy race has mixed itself with the peoples of the lands" (Ezra 9:1).

Counterbalancing the disorders of marriage during this long period are glimpses of marriages that come close to the divinely planned order. That of Ruth — so far as we know it — provides perhaps the most charming example in unusual and apparently unpromising circumstances. The sons of Naomi married foreign wives when they moved to Moab. After their premature death, Ruth, the widow of Mahlon (4:10), insists on accompanying her mother-in-law on the return journey to Bethlehem: "Your people shall be my people and your God my God" (1:16). Naomi, cleverly taking advantage of the Levirate law to secure a fresh husband for Ruth, first introduces her to Boaz and then arranges the night meeting which leads to their marriage. Boaz is no unwilling victim of the stratagem but readily gives his consent to Ruth: "You have made this last kindness greater than the first, in that you have not gone after young men, whether poor or rich. . . . I will do for you all that you ask" (3:10f.). In this "foreign" marriage the usual pattern is broken, for even before the marriage is contracted Ruth commits herself to Israel's God.

The marriage of Ezekiel, though sad in its outcome, seems to have been a sound and happy one from the brief reference in the prophecy. When the time comes for God to take Ezekiel's wife from him as a harsh prophetic symbol, God himself refers to her as "the delight of your eyes" (24:16), just as the temple which was to be destroyed was for Israel. Perhaps the hardest of all the many hard things that Ezekiel had to do in the course of his ministry was to refrain from any outward mourning for his dead wife: "Sigh, but not aloud; make no mourning for the dead. . . . So I spoke to the people in the morning, and at evening my wife died. And on the next morning I did as I was commanded" (Ezek. 24:17f.).

Proverbs has many critical things to say about women, as about all kinds of people both male and female. Often wives seem to be in view: "It is better to live in a desert land than with a contentious and fretful woman" (21:19). Often wives are specifically mentioned: "A wife's quarreling is a continual dripping of rain" (19:13). Yet, in the main, a positive attitude is shown to the wife: "A good wife is the crown of her husband" (12:4); "He who finds a wife finds a good thing" (18:22); "A prudent wife is from the Lord"

(19:14). The good wife is extolled in 31:10ff. She is the true help-meet who cares excellently for material things but contributes also in those that are intellectual (31:26) and spiritual (31:30). She thus helps to set marriage on a firm and durable foundation. Ecclesiastes, even if with a typical touch of cynicism, endorses the possibility of a successful marriage by advising readers to "enjoy life with the wife whom you love, all the days of your vain life" (9:9). The Song of Songs hymns the love of man and woman in words that no one can easily forget: "I am my beloved's and my beloved is mine" (6:3); "Many waters cannot quench love, neither can floods drown it. If a man offered for love all the wealth of his house, it would be utterly scorned" (8:7).

We may still discern the judgment of God in the marriages of the period from the desert wanderings to the exile and beyond. Mistakes avenge themselves by introducing new and painful problems. David cannot escape the stern consequences of his adultery (even though it is forgiven) nor can the weakness of Solomon in taking foreign brides go unrequited. Sometimes God imposes special penalties: David loses his first child by Bathsheba (2 Sam. 12:14); Solomon's kingdom suffers disruption after his death (1 Kings 11:26-12:20); Elijah announces the doom of the house of Ahab (1 Kings 19:15ff.); and the terrible end of Jezebel is similarly prophesied (1 Kings 19:23f.). For the most part, however, things simply follow their natural course. One sin leads to another and the whole process carries with it an almost intolerable burden of human pain and anguish.

Yet the grace of God still reigns in the midst of disobedience and disaster. Nathan declares pardon to David (2 Sam. 12:13). God grants one tribe to the descendants of Solomon instead of taking away the whole kingdom; execution of the penalty is also postponed until after Solomon's death (1 Kings 11:12f.). God similarly postpones judgment on the house of Ahab when the king humbles himself before him (1 Kings 21:27ff.). Nor does marriage itself go down before the assaults of human misuse and transgression. Good or bad, orderly or disorderly, lawful or unlawful, marriage as God's purpose for human life persists under every strain and shock, carrying with it the hope of redemption and renewal as God works out his promise to bring salvation through the child of the woman.

27

Within this context we again see God's sovereignty in marriage. Samson, for all his faults and follies, is born through God's intervention in the lives of Monoah and his wife (Judges 13:2ff.). God sends a special and unexpected blessing upon Hannah and her husband Elkanah with the gift of the child Samuel (1 Sam. 1:19ff.). Above all, God surprisingly chooses two unusual women to play important roles not only in the history of Israel but also in his own history of reconciliation for Israel and the world. The one is the alien Ruth, whom God in spite of his own law against foreign marriages incorporates into the ancestry of David and the Messiah Jesus. The other is the adulterous Bathsheba, whose second son Solomon, in spite of the sin of his parents, is sovereignly chosen to be David's successor, so that by divine favor Bathsheba, too, has a place in the royal and messianic line (see Matt. 1:6, where she is not named directly, as Ruth is in verse 5, but described as "the wife of Uriah the Hittite"). God does not condone the breaking of his will by his human creatures. Yet he can providentially bring human transgressions within the sovereignty of his saving will. Hence, even through the marital disorder of the race the restoration of order is pursued and promoted.

3. THE HUSBAND OF ISRAEL

Foreign marriages, whether through polygamy, adultery, or divorce, almost always carry with them the possibility, and usually the actuality, of apostasy from God and a fall into idolatry. Innumerable instances, some of which have just been quoted, prove this to be true. Infidelity in marriage stands very closely related to infidelity in commitment to God. If this be true, however, idolatry can easily be viewed as itself a form of adultery, i.e., infidelity in the covenant relationship to God. The covenant is a kind of marriage. God has sought out a partner and established a mutual bond: "I will be their God and they shall be my people" (Jer. 31:33). To break this bond is to be guilty of adulterous unfaithfulness by the transfer of love and allegiance to another.

The prophets develop this interpretation of the relation between God and Israel in a whole series of incidents and highly metaphorical addresses which incidentally throw a good deal of new theological light on marriage itself. Isaiah 54 sums up this whole approach when it tells the returning exiles in simple language: "For your Maker is your husband, the Lord of hosts is his name" (v. 5). We should note, of course, that in making statements of this kind Isaiah and the other prophets are not just trying to make God intelligible by portraying him according to the familiar reality of a human husband. To do so would more likely give a distorted view. They are certainly beginning with the broken relationship which so greatly resembles the broken or shaken relationship in many human marriages. In their prophetic messages, however, they then go on to present God as the almost incredible divine husband who deals with the situation, not as one would expect from human husbands, but with his own sovereign grace and gracious sovereignty.

The portrayal of God as the husband of Israel goes back beyond the exilic period to the eighth-century prophet Hosea. Here it takes the form of a parable that is enacted by God's command in the prophet's own life. Hosea is told to take to wife a woman who is a prostitute, just as Israel is in her abandoning God for all kinds of other deities. He obeys God and marries Gomer. The three children of the marriage are given the prophetic names Jezreel, Not Pitied, and Not my People in token of God's judgment on Israel. In spite of the marriage and the children, Gomer continues in her old ways and lives an adulterous life. She eventually leaves Hosea and falls into slavery. At God's command Hosea does not cease to love her in spite of her infidelity, her shameless manner of life, and the despicable position to which she reduces herself. In expression of this love he buys her back for silver and barley and pledges her to new fidelity: "You must dwell as mine for many days. . .so will I also be to you" (Hos. 1-3:3).

The point of Hosea's parabolic experience, driven home in the magnificent poetry of chapter 2, needs little exposition. God in grace has chosen Israel to be his people even though she does not deserve the honor. He has made a binding covenant with her that is comparable to the marriage bond. He will be her God — the election — and she shall be his people — the promise and the command. But unworthy Israel, preferring to go her own way, despises the honor, disobeys the command, and breaks the covenant. She displays the same infidelity as an unfaithful spouse. God lets her take this course. He lets her follow her desires and accept the offers of other suitors: "I will go after my lovers, who give me my bread and my water" (Hos. 2:5). He does not give her the chance to break away from the path of hardship and exile which this entails. Yet he adopts this procedure, not in harshness or anger but in love, not to punish but to restore, not to put away but to win back. The love of God is the patient, faithful, enduring love that Hosea is called upon to show: "I will allure her, and bring her into the wilderness, and speak tenderly to her" (2:14). God looks ahead to the time when this unfaithful wife, bought back by a love that far transcends erotic attraction, will say again, "My husband," and the marriage that seemed to be irreparably broken will be solidly and permanently established: "I will betroth you to me for ever, I will betroth you to me in righteousness and in justice, in steadfast love, and in mercy. I will betroth you to me in faithfulness; and you shall know the Lord" (2:19f.).

Perhaps the only other prophet who can develop the theme with the same depth of personal feeling is Ezekiel. As we have noted, his prophetic ministry demands the sudden loss of his wife. This death serves as a sign that Judah will also lose the delight of her eyes, the temple. But behind this stated meaning stands the suggestion, at least, that in giving up Judah and Jerusalem to ruthless destruction at the hands of the Babylonians, God is also suffering the loss of his wife, the "delight of his eyes." Because of her offences, he is prepared to do this without outward display of grief or mourning. Israel, both north and south, has gone to such a length of adultery (i.e., idolatry) that even—or precisely—in his love and mercy God will no longer refrain from allowing judgment to fall. God has adopted Israel as a foundling child of dubious ancestry (16:1ff.). He has come to her when she was "at the age of love." He has plighted his troth and entered into covenant with her. He has raised her to a state of beauty and renown, lavishing upon her blessings that she could never have earned or secured for herself (16:8ff.). But she has now come to trust in her beauty and to practice harlotry with "any passerby" (16:14). The indictment is severe: Israel is an "adulterous wife, who receives strangers instead of her husband" (16:30). The punishment is equally severe: "I will give you into the hand of your lovers. . .and they shall stone you and cut you to pieces. . . . I will make you stop playing the harlot" (16:39). (The picture presented in chapter 23 is even more vivid, explicit, and terrible.) Nevertheless, even though God hardens his heart to punish, he does not renounce his love for his unfaithful wife or allow his own faithfulness to be broken: "Yet I will remember my covenant with you in the days of your youth, and I will establish with you an everlasting covenant" (16:60). God's love is no selfish affection of giving in return for getting. It is not a judicial love that depends on the worthiness of the beloved. It is a forgiving and self-giving love that refuses to be defeated by the resistance of the beloved but steadfastly persists and conquers: "I forgive you all that you have done, says the Lord God" (16:63).

Jeremiah develops much the same theme with the sensitivity that marks his prophetic ministry and writing. Perhaps a little idealistically, he compares the desert period to a honeymoon: "Thus says the Lord, I remember the devotion of your youth, your love as a bride, how you followed me in the wilderness, in a land not sown" (2:2). He then raises the question of whether a man who divorces his wife will later return to her, after she has married another. (The rule of Deut. 24:1-4, as we recall, forbids marriage in such a case.) Certainly an unfaithful wife can exercise no initiative toward a restoration of the original union: "You have played the harlot with many lovers, and would you return to me?" (3:1). Israel, both north and south, has proved unfaithful (3:6ff.). "Surely, as a faithless wife leaves her husband, so you have been faithless to me, O house of Israel" (3:20). Yet as in Hosea and Ezekiel, so in Jeremiah; God is not bound by the law that he prescribed for human marriage. The gracious and enduring love of God far exceeds what the law allows or demands. Having taken Israel as his bride, God displays to her the covenant love which will not abandon her to others or to herself. He is prepared to forgive every injury and insult and to bring about a restoration of the relationship in spite of her every betrayal and disruption of it. If the wife can exercise no initiative, this husband can. Yes, Israel may indeed come back: "Return, faithless Israel, says the Lord. I will not look on you in anger, for I am merciful, says the Lord" (3:12). No more is needed than acknowledgment of guilt. This is made easier by the fact that judgment has come. The adulterous wife can no longer attract lovers to herself but is scorned and repulsed and maltreated by them: "What do you mean that you dress in scarlet, that you deck yourself with ornaments of gold, that you enlarge your eyes with paint? In vain you beautify yourself. Your lovers despise you; they seek your life" (4:30). Unfaithfulness finally leads to a place where no choice remains but to go down to hopeless ruin or to return to the previously unappreciated and rejected marriage.

The bitterness of the experience of punishment and lost attractiveness comes out sharply in Lamentations. Jerusalem, who has become filthy, remembers all the precious things that were hers from days of old (1:7ff.). Awareness of error and guilt increases the bitterness. Israel had turned to lovers but in the hour of need they fail her: "I called to my lovers but they deceived me" (1:19). The only one she can now turn to is the very husband whom she has wronged by her adulteries: "The steadfast love of the Lord never ceases. . . . Great is thy faithfulness!" (3:22f.). For the moment, however, God seems to be aloof and uncaring. As the prophecy of Isaiah 54 puts it, Israel is left for a time "like a wife forsaken and grieved in spirit, like a wife of youth when she is cast off" (v.6). All around Israel sees other people prospering but for herself she has to bear, as it were, "the reproach of. . .widowhood" (54:4). Yet all this will change. God who is Israel's Maker is also her husband (54:5). He has left his people only for a short time and with great and unmerited compassion he will now restore her: "With everlasting love I will have compassion on you. . . .my steadfast love shall not depart from you, and my covenant of peace shall not be removed" (54:8-10). Israel has no right to love of this kind. It surpasses what one normally looks for even in the love of wife or husband. It contains elements of grace and mercy and patience and persistence which represents a new factor so far as ordinary human relationships are concerned. It is wholly positive: a love that will not be deflected, defeated, or destroyed; a love that is stronger than sin as well as death, a solemn and yet also a supremely joyful love: "As the bridegroom rejoices over the bride, so shall your God rejoice over you" (Isa. 62:5).

As we consider this dramatic presentation of the love of God as the husband of Israel, and think about its implications for the love of husband and wife in marriage, we must remember three things.

First, no special significance attaches to this figure of speech in the general prophetic portrayal of the relations between God and

Israel. Some prophets do not use the comparison with marriage at all. Even in those who do, it occupies only a relatively small amount of space. Hosea, for whom it has a shattering significance, still uses his lively poetic imagination to describe the people not only as an unfaithful wife but also as silly doves (7:11), a stubborn heifer (4:16), and even a half-baked cake (7:8). For Hosea, Israel is also a luxuriant vine (10:1) and a refractory child (11:1ff.). Ezekiel can also give very realistic depictions of the actual sins and idolatries committed by the people (see 8:7ff.). Jeremiah, too, uses the metaphor of disobedient children (3:14) and an implied comparison with scattered sheep (3:15) in the very same context in which he speaks of the unfaithful wife. God himself appears not only as the faithful husband of unfaithful Israel but also as the good shepherd (Jer. 23:3; Ezek. 34:11ff.), the father (Isa. 64:8), the liberator (Isa. 40ff.), and the mother (Isa. 66:13). This by no means minimizes the importance of the comparison with marriage; it simply sets it in perspective.

Second, the prophetic understanding of God as the husband of Israel obviously does not conform to the actual situation in normal human marriages. Wives are very seldom neglected orphans whom husbands graciously adopt and then marry in an act of pure generosity. Unfaithfulness to marital commitments occurs no less frequently (and probably much more) on the part of the husband than on that of the wife. Those spouses who do prove to be unfaithful — and large numbers do not — will not necessarily fall into a situation of want and neglect from which they have to be rescued by their former wives or husbands. Only exceptionally do we find in human marriages the forgiving and invincible love which God displays, and when we do come across something comparable, it is just as likely to be the love of the wife as that of the husband. Like Jesus in the parables, the prophets take situations from real life but they adapt and alter them to fit the special situation — also from real life! — of the relation between God and his people, or, more broadly, between God and the whole of his human creation. We must avoid too close an identification between human marriage and the divine marriage.

Nevertheless, third, the difference between divine and human marriage should not blind us to the implied significance that God's action as the husband of Israel has for the healing of human marriage. After all, God acts as he does toward Israel with a view to redemption and restoration. Hence, his action offers some clues at least to the human action which will be demanded for the redemption and restoration of human marriage within the totality of God's saving work. Two partners in marriage have to consider that, in spite of romantic views of one another, both are sinful and therefore their love will also have to be grace on both sides, a love for someone who really does not merit love. Furthermore, when faults manifest themselves, whether the more sensational faults of sexual infidelity and passionate jealousy or the more humdrum ones of impatience, quarrelsomeness, possessiveness, or irresponsibility, will not human love have to manifest the very same qualities of patience and forbearance and persistence and forgiveness which characterize the husband of Israel? Does not the erotic love of marriage, which is right enough in itself and yet also not enough, have to have the further dimensions of agapic love if real marriage is to be established and maintained? In the comparison of God with a husband, is not God the real husband — the real wife, too!—whereas human husbands and wives, as fallen creatures, are hardly more than travesties of what they are meant to be? Do we not learn from Israel what sorry specimens of married partners we really are? Should we not learn from God what it is to be a real partner in marriage? Does God not indicate to us the way of reconciliation and restoration, not merely according to his example, but on the basis of the deeper work of eternal forgiveness and renewal which the metaphor of the husband so vividly depicts? These are the questions that we need to ponder and answer as we consider the significance of the love of Israel's God and husband not only for our salvation in general but also for the restoration of marriage within it.

III

God the Son and Marriage

1. THE LIFE OF THE SON

The history of God with man reaches its uniquely decisive point when God himself comes on the human scene with the incarnation of the word. As the man Jesus of Nazareth, the divine Son enters into the conditions of human life, lives as man, and goes through death and resurrection to accomplish the work of redemption and restoration both for this age and for eternity. In one transcendent yet historical event the judgment, grace, and sovereignty of God combine to bring salvation not only for Israel but for the whole human race. The Son of God hears the judgment, extends the grace of forgiveness and renewal, and does so in an act of divine sovereignty.

This sovereignty expresses itself in the freedom of Jesus with respect to human conditions and institutions, even while the work he came to do takes place within these conditions and institutions and for their restoration. This finds illustration not least of all in marriage. While God works to restore and reestablish human marriage, he shows toward it the same sovereignty as one finds again and again in the story of Israel. Jesus does not oppose or undermine marriage; yet he is not bound to it either.

The virgin birth, foreshadowed in Genesis 3:15 with its specific reference to the seed of the woman, forms the last and the most extraordinary link in a series of unusual births that extends from Isaac to John the Baptist (Luke 1:5ff.). During this period children often come to aging parents, contrary to normal expectations. In some instances God chooses apparently unsuitable mothers, e.g., the foreigner Ruth and the adulteress Bathsheba. But now in the incarnation he sets aside not only marriage (except in a purely formal sense, Matt. 1:18ff.) but also the ordinary process of human reproduction (Luke 1:31ff.) to initiate the work which will undo the fall. "The power of the Most High" brings about this birth of the child that "is set for the fall and rising of many in Israel" (Luke 1:35; 2:34).

Jesus himself, when he grows to manhood, practices the same freedom in his approach to sex and marriage. While the Gospels draw a veil over almost all his early life, they lend no support to the view that he ever marries. This does not mean that he cuts himself off from female society in a strained and anxious asceticism. His relations with women, while governed by his mission, are natural and sympathetic. He makes no effort to set aside the created order by which human life must be lived in the context of man as male and female. He meets the needs of women (Luke 8:43ff.) and accepts their ministrations (Luke 8:2f.). Yet in singlehearted devotion to his mission he refrains from the relationship of marriage, which is the common human lot. His revealing and reconciling work has the highest claim upon his mind and will and emotions and actions. This demands a single life. He therefore lives a single life. In so doing he incidentally, or not so incidentally, removes from male and female celibacy the stigma that attaches to it in some circles, as if humanity could not just as well find fulfilment outside marriage as it more commonly does within it. If it be objected that Jesus could not experience the fulness of human life without experiencing marriage, one should not forget that the eternal and definitive consummation of humanity will in fact be outside human marriage (Mark 12:25).

As Jesus accepts celibacy for himself, not as a preferred lifestyle or an intentional idiosyncracy, but in fulfilment of his mission, so he makes demands upon his disciples which entail a relativizing of the marriage bond. He tells Peter, who is married, to follow him, and at once Peter begins an itinerant life which leads him across Galilee to Jerusalem, then to Samaria and Antioch, and finally across much of the Roman world. He makes the stern and almost impossible statement that if people who come to him do not "hate" their fathers and mothers and *wives* and children and their own lives, they cannot be his disciples (Luke 14:26). In the parable of the banquet to which many of the invited guests refuse to come, the apparently reasonable excuse, "I have married a wife, and therefore I cannot come," is summarily rejected. Undertaking and practicing a higher allegiance even than that of marriage, Jesus expects his followers to do the same.

Nevertheless, revolutionary though all this may sound, Jesus does not oppose or attack marriage. As the Book of Common Prayer so finely puts it, "he adorned and beautified with his presence, and first miracle that he wrought," the marriage in Cana of Galilee (John 2:1ff.). He undoubtedly asks Peter and the others to leave everything and follow him, but he does not order Peter to abandon his wife. In fact, just after the call, he goes to Peter's home and heals his wife's mother, who is suffering from a fever (Mark 1:30f.). Peter certainly leaves all to follow Jesus (Mark 10:28) and this leads him later to engage in extensive missionary and pastoral travel, but far from leaving his wife we learn from Paul that he takes her with him, as other apostles and the brothers of the Lord take their wives, too (1 Cor. 9:5). There is no evidence to suggest that "hating" wives was either meant or taken literally or that Jesus breaks up marriages except where partners differ sharply in their response to himself and his saving work. His mission is a mission of reconciliation, not division. No understanding of his life, or the life to which he calls his disciples, can possibly be correct if it finds in the sovereign freedom of Jesus a disparagement or disruption of marriage.

What, then, does this freedom in relation to marriage mean? It means, first, that commitment to God must have priority over every other commitment. Not even the deep personal commitment of marriage can be allowed to interfere with one's relationship to God. The radical mistake of the human race is that of pushing God into second or third or last place, of putting the will of self in place of the will of God, of giving a higher value to other goals than to the purpose of God. Jesus cuts right across this. If the human situation is to be remedied, the fault has to be exposed and

37

reversed. Jesus must put his divinely commissioned ministry first: "Not as I will, but as thou wilt" (Matt. 26:39). So, too, must his disciples, as the bearers of the good news of salvation accomplished in him. No restoration of order can ever come without the restoration of a right order of relationships in which the relationship to God comes first, even before that of husband and wife.

Yet, second, the restoration of the right order of relationships carries with it the remedying of all other disorders. This is the point: Jesus is *for* marriage, not against it. He can be for it, however, only by being against it in the form in which it is attempted by those who do not put the commitment to God first. Man and woman can never achieve marriage as God intended it if they have their priorities wrong. They cannot achieve it even if the one gives to the other a priority of commitment. The disorder of a wrong relationship to God will thwart their best intentions and all their best efforts at a successful marriage. Primary commitment to God does not compete with a legitimate commitment to marriage. On the contrary, it gives to it both the possibility and the reality that it cannot otherwise have. Jesus displays sovereignty regarding marriage, and enjoins it on others, in order to put marriage back again on a proper foundation by way of a recognition of the all-embracing sovereignty of God over all human life and destiny.

2. THE TEACHING OF THE SON

God the incarnate Son does not have a great deal to say about marriage in his recorded teaching. Of what he does say, only a small part deals directly with the theme. The rest consists of indirect references and allusions with more or less obvious implications. Nevertheless, what we have has to be regarded as highly significant. This applies both to negative sayings on freedom regarding marriage and to positive sayings on the nature and permanence of marriage.

Incidentally, the law in its accusing and convicting function takes on an even sharper edge in the ministry of Jesus than in the Old Testament. This is obviously true in regard to sexuality. The tenth commandment, as we have seen, digs beneath the act of adultery to the initial sin of coveting a neighbor's spouse, whether this results in the act of adultery or not. Jesus digs deeper still. Not merely coveting one's neighbor's spouse but looking with desire at a person of the opposite sex has in it a sinful element that can be called an adultery of the heart (Matt. 5:28). The full implication of this radicalizing of the law would seem to be that erotic love — the love that leads to courtship and marriage as well as to fornication or adultery — can never be completely pure in a fallen race, good though it may be in itself. We must be careful not to misunderstand this. Sexual love is not initially or intrisically wrong or bad or impure, as some ascetics suppose. How can it be? God himself planned and designed it for the creature that he made in his own image both male and female. The fault does not lie with sexuality as such but with the creature which enters into the good and beautiful sexual union that God willed. This creature is now the fallen creature. It brings into all its thoughts and words and acts an element of distortion and corruption. For this reason, even the marriage relation itself can claim no perfection. It does not lie outside the realm of sin. In the very best of circumstances, it needs the divine forgiveness, like all other human relations. How much more so do the errant desires of both the married and the unmarried, whether they lead to errant actions or not! Sexuality is by no means the core of human sin. Like all else human, it is good as created. Yet, also like all else human, it proves to be manifestly sinful as practiced by human sinners.

The story of the woman taken in adultery (John 8:1ff.) provides graphic illustration of both the extent and intensity of human sin. This woman has broken the law outwardly and her accusers ask Jesus whether she should not suffer the penalty of the law. But Jesus shifts the focus from the flagrant transgression of the woman to the inner sinfulness of us all which is its root. Those among her accusers who have no sin are invited to cast the first stone. None of them can take up the challenge. Only a few, perhaps, have committed adultery. But that is not the point. Many more might have had guilty desires in their hearts and can no longer play the hypocrite in the presence of Jesus. Even if they have not, they know only too well that they are guilty of other and no less deadly sins. Beginning with the eldest, they slink away. Nor does Jesus himself condemn the woman. If he has come to bring sin to light, he has also come to forgive and cleanse it. She is to go and not sin again (8:11).

39

When we turn to the specific teaching of Jesus about marriage, we do not discern any obvious chronological sequence. Hence we might group the sayings in the same way as we did the attitude and practice of Jesus in the preceding section. We again begin with the material which exhibits a certain freedom regarding marriage, which refuses to treat it as an overriding absolute in human life, which argues that for some people at least, in virtue of their commitment to God, celibacy can be a better way either temporarily or permanently.

Replying to the question of the Pharisees about divorce (Matt. 19:3ff.), Jesus describes remarriage after divorce as adultery. In an impulsive if not wholly logical train of thought the disciples react at once: "If such is the case of a man with his wife, it is not expedient to marry" (v. 10). To this observation Jesus gives a somewhat enigmatic answer (vv. 11f.). He says, first, that not all people can receive this precept. It can hardly be a matter for general legislation. A gift is needed if a person separated from a former spouse is to live without remarrying. Jesus seems to recognize that marriage is the normal state, which only sin has disrupted and in some cases made more or less impossible. Nevertheless, the gift of a celibate life can be and is given. Life can go on apart from marriage. In some cases celibacy is indeed enforced by birth, accident, or human action. In others a higher allegiance takes precedence over that of marriage. Even ordinary people, including those whose marriages break down but who recognize that marriage is not everything, can become celibate for the sake of God's kingdom. In the world of the fall the redemptive work of God carries with it a service of God — not necessarily a technical ministry but a service according to God's will, by God's appointment, and in God's discipleship — which means that some part of life, if not all, must be lived temporarily or permanently outside the regular patterns of God's created order.

This reminds us of the order of priorities which Jesus demands in the calling of his disciples. What God requires must come before all else, the good as well as the bad. The followers of Jesus must be ready, should he will, to renounce even marriage for the sake of the gospel. They must be ready to obey God and not remarry after separation even though they might plead, as they often do, that they have a right to happiness or to the fulfilment of

40

natural desires. To talk of a right to happiness is to delude oneself. Happiness, when it is attained, is a gift from God and it cannot be attained, nor can human life be fulfilled, where there is conflict with God's stated will or a defiant refusal to see that true happiness and fulfilment lie only in a primary commitment to God's kingdom and righteousness. For God's sake some people may have to forego marriage, some may have to put it in a new perspective, and some who have broken their marriages may have to refrain from remarriage. Marriage is a good thing but it is not "the one thing needful" (Luke 10:42). Hence it may be — and in some instances it may have to be — surrendered.

Along the same lines Jesus, the living and incarnate Son, informs us that marriage belongs only to the temporal order and not to the eternal. The cynical Sadducees, who did not accept the resurrection, confronted Jesus with a false problem in order to ridicule the very idea of a future life. They pressed the Levirate law to the absurd extreme where seven brothers successively marry the same woman without any of them having any children by her. If, however, there is a resurrection, whose wife will she be in the new and everlasting life? (Matt. 22:23ff.). Jesus in his reply disposes of the problem rapidly. In the resurrection people neither marry nor are given in marriage. By God's institution marriage may be the supreme and perfect relationship for man and woman in this life but in the life of the resurrection, when we are "like angels in heaven" (Matt. 22:30), God has for us an even more perfect relationship which cannot be described in terms of our present life on earth. Marriage, for all its high significance, has an eschatological limit. Married partners need not be afraid that they will lose the precious thing they already have. They will no longer be married, but in God they will have a more wonderful relationship that transcends the very best that marriage could ever offer, let alone what it can now offer in the sinful situation after the fall.

The limits that the primacy of God and the nature of eternal life place on marriage do not reduce its central importance in the message of God the Son. Taking up the thought of God as the husband of Israel, Jesus compares his own mission to a wedding. When the disciples of the ascetic John the Baptist ask why the disciples of Jesus do not fast when they and the Pharisees do, he poses a counterquestion: "Can the wedding guests mourn so long as the bridegroom is with them?" (Mark 2:18ff.). A time will come when the groom will be absent and then there will be fasting. But this is the time of the presence of the bridegroom. In Jesus, God has come to claim his bride for himself and to do the work which will establish the marriage as one that is solid and enduring. The hour of this work and coming is an hour of rejoicing. The Baptist himself understands this, according to the witness of John's Gospel, when he says that "he who has the bride is the bridegroom; the friend of the bridegroom, who stands and hears him, rejoices greatly at the bridegroom's voice; therefore this joy of mine is now full" (John 3:29).

The comparison with a wedding occurs also in some of the parables of Jesus, though not necessarily with any direct implications for marriage itself. Thus, the kingdom of heaven is like a marriage feast that a king gives for his son. Some of the invited guests refuse to come and even manhandle those who bring the invitation. Among those who finally accept is a person who does not have on a wedding garment. The primacy attaching to the kingdom seems to be the main point of this extended comparison. But why is the marriage feast chosen as the symbol? We must not be too fanciful here. Yet we might at least suggest that marriage holds such a place of primacy among human relationships that even the most pressing of human concerns cannot excuse the refusal to attend the wedding banquet (Matt. 25:1ff., but note the relativizing of earthly marriage by the divine marriage in Luke 14:20).

The parable of the ten virgins again uses the metaphor of the wedding (Matt. 25:1ff.). This time the thrust is eschatological. The reference of the parable is to the Christ who both comes and comes again. The bridegroom will be coming at some unspecified hour and his people must be ready to greet him with lamps burning. The bridegroom himself constitutes the center of attention rather than the wedding feast. He will take with him to the feast those who are prepared and he will shut out those who are not. No particular inferences can be drawn for human marriage, but the choice of the metaphor again emphasizes its high significance in the divine plan for the creature.

The eucharistic sayings include an interesting reference to the future banquet which will occur the next time that Jesus drinks wine with his disciples (Matt. 26:29; Mark 14:25; Luke 22:18). The disciples are those whom Jesus has appointed to eat and drink at his table in his kingdom (Luke 22:30). The Gospels do not specifically describe this so-called messianic banquet as a marriage feast, but Revelation seems to equate the two when it speaks of the marriage supper of the Lamb (Rev. 19:9; see also 21:9). If earthly marriage does not last into eternal life, the marriage of God and his people does. It is now portrayed as the marriage of Christ and the church. Here is the perfect relationship — the relationship with and in Christ — which replaces the highest of earthly relationships transcendently and eternally.

We learn from all this that as God made man in his own image, so he made earthly marriage in the image of his own eternal marriage with his people. Marriage, for all its inadequacy, can serve as a comparison for God's relationship to Israel and Christ's to the church because it draws from this relationship its own essential character. This means that we are not to understand the true reality of God's union with us in terms of marriage but *vice versa*. We know the true reality of marriage from God's way of dealing with us and the inward and eternal fellowship that he establishes. Marriage in the situation of human disorder does not measure up to the divine intention for marriage. But the will of God expressed by Jesus is that it should do so.

The expression of this will comes in the Sermon on the Mount (Matt. 5:31f.) and then more extensively in the answer to the testing question of the Pharisees about divorce (Mark 10:2ff.; Matt. 19:3ff.; cf. Luke 16:18). In the version in Mark the Pharisees want to embarrass Jesus. They are probably trying to get him to commit himself to either easy or harder divorce and thereby to align himself with a particular party. Jesus, as he so often does, replies first by putting a counterquestion: "What did Moses command you?" (Mark 10:3). The Pharisees quote the law of Deuteronomy 24:1, which allows divorce for "some indecency" and does not forbid the remarriage of either of the divorced partners, only their subsequent remarriage to one another. Jesus then springs a surprise. The Mosaic law of divorce, he says, came only as a concession to a hardhearted people. God has not gone back on his original intention that one man should be so joined to one woman that they become one. No one should dare to separate what God has joined together.

Very plainly this seems to be saying that for Jesus and those who follow him, whose stony hearts have been replaced by hearts of flesh (Ezek. 36:26), the Old Testament law is withdrawn and the created order of marriage comes back into full force. The sayings about remarriage after divorce back up this reading. In Mark 10 the disciples pursue the topic "in the house" (v. 10). They receive from Jesus the unequivocal and uncompromising reply: "Whoever divorces his wife and marries another commits adultery against her (the male has no privilege); and if she divorces her husband, she commits adultery" (v. 11). The saying in the Sermon on the Mount, which transcends the Mosaic law ("It was also said. . . but I say unto you"), is to the same effect: "Every one who divorces his wife. . .makes her an adulteress; and whoever marries a divorced woman commits adultery" (Matt. 5:32). So, too, is the saying in Luke 16:18: "Every one who divorces his wife and marries another commits adultery, and he who marries a woman divorced from her husband commits adultery."

The saying in Matthew 5:32, however, contains a puzzling exceptive clause: "except on the ground of unchastity." We find the same exception in Matthew 19:9, where Jesus in his answer to the Pharisees says: "Whoever divorces his wife, except for unchastity, and marries another, commits adultery." The puzzling element is that while, on the one hand, the Mosic law is obviously transcended (5:31) and the Mosaic concession is no less obviously withdrawn (19:8), on the other hand, the legal provision is apparently restored in what is perhaps a narrower yet still indefinite form.

Many Christians explain the situation in this way. Mark 10 enunciates again the principle (or ideal) of marriage for the unfallen human creature. But today as yesterday, even for those who belong to the people of God, sin brings such great problems and tensions and complexities into married life that they cannot attain the ideal and some relief has to be given by Jesus as it was by Moses. The sayings in Matthew offer this relief in qualification of the declaration of the complete indissolubility of marriage in Mark.

Yet do they? Two difficulties face this interpretation. First, "unchastity" is not clearly defined. For Gentile Christians, especially those converted recently from different forms of paganism, it might cover things such as bigamy or incest which invalidate a marriage from the very outset, so that justifiable nullification is the issue, not divorce. Second, no plain mandate for remarriage occurs in any of the sayings — Matthew 19:9 comes closest — so that even if many circumstances can arise which make separation wise or necessary, divorce in the full sense, with the freedom to remarry during the lifetime of the original partner, does not seem to come unequivocally into the picture.

The experience of the woman of Samaria in John 4 might be considered in this connection. When Jesus asks her to fetch her husband, she gives the evasive answer: "I have no husband" (4:16f.). Jesus is not deceived. He acknowledges that she has told the truth: "You are right in saying, 'I have no husband' " (4:17). But the reason that her answer is true is that she has had five husbands already and the man she now has is not her husband (4:18). We do not know the details of the woman's marital history. But in view of the legitimacy of remarriage for widows, it seems fairly obvious that her previous marriages had ended in some form of separation or divorce, unless she had simply given herself to a life of multiple adultery. In the eyes of Jesus, however, a succession of remarriages after divorce amounts to much the same thing as multiple adultery. The man she now lives with, whether there has been a form of marriage or not, is not her husband.

Four points may be made in conclusion. First, none of the Gospels offers the kind of blank check for divorce and remarriage which many Christian preachers, teachers, and counsellors offer today and many Christians who run into marital problems are ready to take. Second, the story of the encounter with the Pharisees seems to make no final sense if Jesus finishes up by endorsing the Mosaic law which at first he so bravely describes as a concession and replaces with the original creation principle. Third, the incarnate Son undoubtedly champions — and intends to champion — the divinely instituted permanence and indissolubility of the union of man and woman. People can, of course, put asunder what God has joined together, but they are well advised not to do so. Fourth and finally, Jesus has not come simply to announce a continuation of the bondage to sin which explains and validates the Mosaic concession. He has come to bring a new freedom, not for divorce, but for marriage. He does not give a new and stricter law to his disciples, laying on them a burden that they cannot carry. Instead, he opens up for them the possibility of doing willingly and effectively that which previously, even out of the strictest sense of duty, they could not do, or could do only with great difficulty and at great cost. How does he do this?

3. THE SAVING WORK OF THE SON

To answer the question at the end of the preceding section we have to look beyond the example and the teaching of Jesus to his work of redemption and restoration. God the Son comes into the world as the heavenly bridegroom, rescuing or establishing his own marriage in face of the infidelity of his spouse or bride. To accomplish this task, which will carry with it the reinstitution of earthly marriage, he does two things: he bears the cost of human unfaithfulness and he breaks its power. In these two ways he wins, or wins back, to himself a people that can finally be united to him in endless union. He also makes it possible for this people to realize to some degree on earth the creaturely copy of this union in human marriage.

First, he bears the cost or carries the penalty of sin. He takes to himself all the guilt that we incur before God by sinful thoughts and words and acts. He carries for us all the sin that we commit in our marriages. He bears this guilt and bears it away, so that we can stand before God pardoned, acquitted, forgiven, and justified. He breaks the chain of sin, so that while some of its practical consequences remain, it loses its power to cause lasting disorder, confusion, or conflict. He removes from the lives of those who believe in him the element of cumulative judgment. He brings liberation from the past and freedom for the new present and the new future.

What are the results of this vicarious bearing of the penalty of sin by the divine Son? Too often we rejoice in its eternal truth and overlook its immediate implications. This gives to Christianity an air of unreality which is totally misleading. As believers in Christ we are forgiven sinners. What does this mean for marriage? It can and should make all the difference. We do not have to suffer forever the consequences of our past misdeeds. We can and must forgive one another as the Lord instructs us (Matt. 6:14f.) and as God for Christ's sake has forgiven us (Eph. 4:32). We recognize that, being sinners, we need forgiveness from one another as we do from God, and by the same token we need to forgive one another. And forgiveness is now possible. We do not need to carry around the burden of grudges, fears, jealousies, suspicions, hurts, resentments, and hostilities which wreck so many marriages. Reconciliation with God — the first step of restoration as the break with God was the first step of disintegration — carries with it the reconciliation with one another to which even the worst and deepest and broadest of human conflicts must yield.

Forgiveness of the past opens the door to the future. If the divine Son has carried the cost and penalty of our sin, sin is a defeated foe. Yet it can still be a powerful one. It will not let go easily. A single incident of emotional reconciliation in the light of the cross will not solve every problem of marriage or of any other human relationship. New sources of hurt and irritation will constantly arise. New acts of pride, willfulness, folly, and selfishness will bring new distortions and new crises to the marital union. Yet these can no longer inflict lasting or mortal wounds on marriage partners who know that as forgiven sinners they must also forgive one another. Living with *divine* reconciliation as a constant fact in human life means living with *mutual* reconciliation as a constant fact. This makes indissoluble union a practical and attainable goal even for sinners. The need for a concession to hardheartedness will no longer arise, for the sinners are forgiven sinners. Even if a serious rift should occur, even if one partner should relapse into an unforgiving attitude, this does not mean that forgiveness has to fail on both sides. Forgiven sinners may sometimes ignore or forget the implications of their own forgiveness, but if they truly know themselves as forgiven sinners they cannot ultimately refuse forgiveness. That is why a new future opens up for Christian marriage.

Second, the Son of God, in integral fulfilment of the same saving work, breaks the power of sin as well as bearing its penalty. How does he do this? By simply bearing the penalty, one might reply. Does not forgiveness generate forgiveness? Does not God's reconciling of us to himself entail our reconciliation with one another? Indeed it does, yet how? The mere fact that the cost or penalty is vicariously transferred from us to him does not seem to alter the power of sin nor to alter those who commit the sin. Why should the removing of the penalty be also the breaking of the power? Do we have here only the attractive possibility of a renewal by psychological response? Is there any certainty that this possibility will ever be a practical reality? While it may be true that we can forgive one another and be reconciled to one another so long as we grasp and apply the implications of our own forgiveness and reconciliation with God, is there any compelling reason why this should take place? Does the saving work of the Son make any real and necessary difference when it comes to the business of daily conduct, whether in marriage or in anything else?

These questions all boil down to the one question: How is it that the vicarious work of God the Son, as a bearing of the cost and penalty of sin, also breaks the power of sin? The answer is that it does this because this work has for us the meaning of our own death and resurrection in the dying and rising again of Christ. When Jesus died on the cross, not only did he cancel our sin and guilt, but we the sinners died in and with this representative of ours. Similarly, when Jesus was buried and then rose again the third day from the dead, not only did our old life go down to death and burial with him but we the sinners were also raised to newness of life in him. This is the truth that Paul states so well in Romans 6:3ff. (and more briefly in Gal. 2:20). This is also the message of Jesus: Life must be lost for his sake if it is to be saved (Mark 8:35); a new life is given (John 3:3ff.) and a transition from death to life takes place in him (John 5:24).

In bearing the cost of sin, Christ so closely identifies himself with us that we die when he dies. Our old life comes to an end. Before God it no longer exists. Judgment has been passed and executed upon it. The fulfilment of this death, of course, will come only with physical dissolution or with Christ's coming again at the end of the age. But already it is a reality because God reputes us to be dead in the death of Jesus his Son. In our interim life, between the entry into Christ's work in faith and the end that is ahead of us, we are thus to live as those who are dead to sin, to our old selves, to the sinful past. We are to live a life of denial of self, or, as Paul puts it, of mortification.

Though mortification is not a hopeless exercise in self-reform, though it is a putting off of that which already in the true reality of God is past and done with, it is not, of course, an easy process. As

Luther reminds us, the old Adam (or Eve) does not die willingly. It struggles to stay alive. Its head has been struck off but it still lashes out and strikes and wounds. Even though it has no future, it can still affect the present. In marriage it stirs up the old sins of selfishness, annoyance, discord, illicit desire, and jealousy, with the accompanying reactions of resentment, retaliation, obstinacy, and a resolute unreadiness to forgive. Not for a moment dare Christians forget that in Christ, where their true being now is, they are dead to sin, and that those who have died are freed from sin so that it need not and should not reign any longer in their mortal bodies (Rom. 6:7ff.). Christ by his vicarious death has broken the power of sin — notwithstanding its temporary virulence — because in and with him our life of sin has ended. What we now do as sinners we do not do as our true selves. Sinful acts and attitudes are the things that are to be put off as part of the past, which is not just forgiven but over. Between the time that remains to us before his coming, or our going to be with him, we are to set aside these works of darkness, forgiving one another for them, recognizing that they are not works of the true self, seeking forgiveness for them when we ourselves commit them.

Mortification, of course, is negative. Putting off things, or ceasing to do them, leaves a vacuum. It needs to be complemented by something positive. We could not even speak of it without presupposing that the bad things would at least be replaced by their opposites. The saving work of Christ, as we have seen, includes this replacement. In his work for us the incarnate Son of God both died and rose again. Hence we who believe in him not only die but also rise again with him. As this old life comes to an end, a new life begins: "As Christ was raised from the dead by the glory of the Father, we too might walk in newness of life" (Rom. 6:4). Our entry into the fulness of this newness of life will come only at the resurrection of the dead, when this physical body yields to the spiritual body and this perishable nature puts on the imperishable. Nevertheless, the newness of life is already a reality because God counts his people to be alive in and with the risen Jesus. Living between the entry into this new life in faith and its fulfilment at the resurrection, we are to live as those who are alive to God, to the new being in him, to the righteous future. We are to live the life of renewal, or, as Paul puts it in 2 Corinthians 5:17, of new creation.

This again is a difficult task. Constantly hampered by the old and only too familiar self, we find it hard to believe that we are really new, let alone to put this newness into daily practice. How easily it all seems to be an illusion or a purely theoretical truth! Yet it is no illusion nor is it mere theory. We must accept it in faith as indeed the real truth about ourselves. What we now are before God, we are in Christ. We must work out this truth in daily conduct, as God expects and requires of us. In our marriages, for example, we are now new husbands and new wives. The former things have gone; all things are made new. Living as God's children adopted by him because we are in his Son, we no longer find it so important to get and to rule; we want to give more and to serve more. We see that agapic love applies also and precisely in marriage. Selfishness and bad temper and evil desire and jealousy do not belong to the new life of the children of God. Forbearance and forgiveness do. Upsets will come. Circumstances will often seem to conspire against us. Crises will occur that bring discord and confusion. Ancient problems will again rear their ugly heads. Old hurts will revive, old faults reassert themselves, and old resentments gain an entrance. Differences of judgment and opinion will come, often about trivial matters that suddenly take on enormous proportions, sometimes about very serious matters which threaten to thrust us into an impasse where tempers run short and reconciliation seems to be unattainable. The escape hatch of divorce constantly presents itself as a tempting solution: Why struggle and suffer? Why endure the pain of friction? Why not seek release and a chance of possible happiness somewhere else? Yet, over all such situations of tension and turmoil lies the simple truth: You are no longer those dead people fighting those dead battles and seeking those dead solutions. By God's gracious work of resurrection in Jesus Christ you are new people with a new peace and a new basis of reconciliation. You are the children of God. You are living the new life of God's new creation. You love now, not just with the erotic love of creation, but with the kind of love with which God himself loved you, the love that goes the second mile, the love that persists even though at first it meets with little or no response, the love that forgives and forbears. The past has gone. Even in disagreement you can agree to disagree, leaving it for God to decide those things that you cannot decide for yourselves, mutually deferring to one another in a higher agreement that transcends disagreement. You have been crucified with Christ. You live, but in a very real and practical sense, and not just in some mystical abstraction, it is Christ who now lives in you. The life that you now live is the life that is lived in faith in the Son of God, who loved you and gave himself for you (Gal. 2:20). It is the life in which all thoughts and words and acts and attitudes and relations are in the process of being conformed to the image of Christ by the transformation deriving from inner renewal.

Have we the power really to live out this mortification and renewal as those who in Christ are dead to sin and alive to God? In ourselves we certainly do not. This being so, is it not all still a dream — a beautiful dream, but a dream all the same? Is it not an illusion to think that the power of sin is broken if, even though we are dead to sin, we have no strength to resist its dying strokes in this interim life but still live as the old sinners we were instead of the new people we now are?

This is a searching question. It has about it an air of plausibility, especially when we consult our continuing problems in marriage and in other human relationships. Yet in the last analysis it has no substance. It rests on a misunderstanding. For while it is true that we ourselves, even as God's new creation, do not have in ourselves the power to live out our death to sin and our rising again to God, this does not mean that no power at all exists for this purpose. God himself has in fact provided us with the necessary power for mortification and renewal. He has done this through his word and through the faith which it engenders. Indeed, as God the Holy Spirit, he himself is the power.

Paul puts this well in Romans 7:6: "We serve. . .in the new life of the Spirit." The Holy Spirit, the giver of life, is he who makes us new people in and with the rising again of Christ. The law of the new life is that of the Spirit of life (Rom. 8:2). Living according to the Spirit, we set our minds on the things of the Spirit (8:5). We are in the Spirit as the Spirit dwells in us (8:9). Life is given to our mortal bodies through the indwelling Spirit (8:11). By the Spirit we may truly put to death the deeds of the body (8:13). Led by the Spirit we are God's children and enjoy already a foretaste of the glorious liberty of the children of God (8:14, 21). Freedom from the old self and freedom to live the new life in Christ is given to us to exercise in every tangled relationship of life. It is ours to exercise in marriage as we follow the directions of the Holy Spirit and experience for ourselves his regenerating and life-renewing ministry.

IV

God the Holy Spirit
and Marriage

1. THE DIRECTIONS OF THE SPIRIT

What does it mean to be led by the Spirit so that we may know the power by which to die to sin and live to God? Is it a purely subjective experience as some people have thought? Do individual believers get direct personal prompting from the Spirit for specific situations? Do they receive an inner signal that this and not that is the right course to take? Will the leading of the Spirit always be different for different people in different situations, so that no objective guidance can be sought or expected?

The existence of holy scripture, and especially of the New Testament, obviously seems to refute such interpretations. As God the Son raised up special disciples (or apostles) to be with him through his ministry and to be the primary witnesses of his life and death and resurrection, so the Holy Spirit moved these disciples and others to give an authentic oral and written testimony to the work of Christ both for us and in us. Unquestionably, specific circumstances will always differ in the lives and experiences of different believers, so that the application of the leading and empowering of the Holy Spirit will indeed take different forms. Nevertheless, the general guidance of the Spirit constitutes an objective reality which exists permanently in the apostolic writings and in the ministry of the church as it is based upon these and uses them as an authoritative norm.

Applied to marriage this objective reality takes the form of biblical directions or injunctions for Christians by which the will of the Spirit is known and for the implementing of which the power of the Spirit is available. These directions are not laws in the Old Testament sense. They do not carry with them any physical or financial penalties for infraction. Eternal life or death does not depend on their perfect observance. Christ has died and risen again to atone for sin and to open up the way to everlasting life with God. No legalistic tension need arise as we look at the directions. We are not asked to do them out of a sense of duty. We are not required to find from within ourselves the resources for their observance. They will undoubtedly convict us of sin when we wilfully disregard or disobey them, but our incidental failures to keep them will not displace us from God's eternal favor nor form a definitive hindrance to the living of the new life of righteousness and sanctification. As believers, we come to them with an inner desire to go where the Spirit leads. Hence we welcome his directions. We have a prior willingness to follow them. Here is the path to the life of freedom in which we can truly be what we truly are, those who have newness of life in God the Son, who are thus by adoption the new children of God the Creator and Father, and who have God the Holy Spirit dwelling within them as the basis and power of sanctification.

None of this means, of course, that we can take the directions of the Spirit lightly. Indeed, disobeying them can and should bring us under the discipline of the church, though this, of course, is designed to correct and to help, not to judge and to punish (1 Cor. 5:2ff.). Disobeying them also incurs the displeasure of God, whose will it is that we should live our new lives in Christ in conformity with his own design. Disobeying them also constitutes a setback to sanctification and brings us into the absurd contradiction of turning the new freedom to do God's will into the old and illusory freedom of doing what we like — a repetition of the mistake of our first parents at the fall. The work that Christ has done *for* us and that the Holy Spirit is doing *in* us carries, in fact, an inner imperative of its own. We are not confronted by an external command. We live with an inner compulsion. As the new people we now are, we have to will what God wills, and we delight to do so. What this is, he shows to us in and by the directions that the Holy Spirit offers through the apostolic witness.

A first direction, given by the apostle Paul, is that incest has no more place in the Christian church than it had in ancient Israel. Writing to the Corinthians, the apostle complains that "there is immorality among you, and of a kind that is not found even among pagans; for a man is living with his father's wife" (1 Cor. 5:1). The Holy Spirit will lead God's people away from this kind of relationship and not into it. Working out the marital implications of newness of life in Christ cannot involve experimentation with unusual relationships in the name of a supposed new freedom from law under the rule of grace. Indeed, this type of relationship is so plainly contrary to the leading and the inner compulsion of the Spirit that the church must feel deep pain if it occurs, and exercise the discipline of removal on those responsible. Only church members who either have no conception of what God's will for marriage is or are deliberately rejecting it can engage in such conduct. (Whether or not incest includes all the relations covered by the prohibitions of the Old Testament has been a matter of debate in the church. Many people have thought that it does.)

A second direction, also given by Paul, concerns adultery and fornication. In this respect the apostle specifically endorses the seventh commandment, which receives similar endorsement in other New Testament passages as well (Matt. 5:27; 19:18; Rom. 13:9). Adulterers, he declares, will not inherit God's kingdom (1 Cor. 6:9). Why not? Does not Christ's forgiveness extend to adulterers, too? Indeed it does ("such were some of you," 6:11). But adultery as the act of non-Christians, or even as the temporary relapse of Christians, differs widely from a wilful continuation in adultery on the part of believers. Christ does not say to the woman caught in the act of adultery: "Neither do I condemn you; go, and if you are caught again and again and again, it will not make any difference, you will still be forgiven." Possibly she might sin again and be forgiven again, but if she defiantly goes back to adultery as a way of life, the situation obviously changes. The Holy Spirit does not lead into adultery but away from it. Hence the new life in Christ for which the Spirit empowers us will be one in which adultery has no place. The same applies to fornication: "The body

55

is not meant for immorality, but for the Lord, and the Lord for the body" (1 Cor. 6:13). The believer is a member of Christ in the union which is the prototype of the marital union itself. But to give oneself to a prostitute is to become one body with her in a betrayal of the union with Christ and a dreadful travesty of the holy union of marriage: "The two shall become one" (6:15). Immorality of this kind also involves a unique sin against one's own body as the temple or dwelling-place of the Holy Spirit (6:19). With adultery it belongs to the old and dead life that lay under the dominion of sin. Christians who have been given a new life and the power to live this life and the inner desire to do God's will are warned against allowing the old Adam and the old Eve to come to life again and to find cheap and destructive gratification in such immoral acts. The new man and the new woman in Christ have a freedom from them which is also a freedom for true and constructive joy and fulfilment in marriage. Even within marriage, of course, the old nature may seek to reassert itself and produce a kind of married fornication (even to the point of rape). The mere institution does not guarantee renewal in the Spirit, as examples from the Old Testament have shown. The renewal has to come from the marriage partners themselves, and for them the direction of the empowering Spirit takes the following form: "That each one of you know how to take a wife for himself in holiness and honor, not in passion of lust like heathen who do not know God. . . . For God has not called us for uncleanness, but in holiness" (1 Thess. 4:4f., 7). Led and inwardly impelled by the Spirit, the new man and the new woman can and should achieve a union of true love, not of conventionalized lust.

In a third direction Christians are plainly told to marry only Christians. Unions with unbelievers have no more prospect of success than those of Jews with Gentiles in the Old Testament. The Holy Spirit again uses Paul to make this point. Addressing the confused Corinthians, he does it bluntly: "Do not be mismated with unbelievers" (2 Cor. 6:14). He gives the reason in a series of vivid rhetorical questions: What partnership is there between good and bad, what fellowship between light and darkness, what accord between Christ and Belial, what agreement between the temple of God and idols (6:14ff.)? These questions bring out the inherent, deep-seated, and insuperable incompatibility that such mismatings involve, for in the ultimate sense, "What has a believer in common with an unbeliever?" (6:15). Paul rounds off the argument with some Old Testament quotations which teach the exclusiveness of the people or family of God and their consequent need to be separate: "As God said. . .'I will be their God, and they shall be my people. Therefore come out from them, and be separate from them, says the Lord. . .and I will be a father to you' " (6:16ff.). This separation does not mean withdrawal from the world, for it is there that Christians must bear witness not only with words but also with their new and holy lives (see 1 Cor. 5:9ff.). What it does mean is that they must not enter into such intimate relationships with non-Christians as that of marriage. These relationships carry with them an inbuilt incompatibility at the deepest level. Contamination with ungodly modes of thought and speech and action, and the triumphant resurgence of the old life, may well be the result. Or the tension may become so intolerable that the relationship is overthrown and its original purpose is thwarted.

This particular direction, like that against adultery, plainly adopts and restates an Old Testament law, namely, the law against mixed marriages. The Old Testament prohibition, with its references to the deities of the nations around Israel, will have for many people an outdated and old-fashioned ring. Christians today are not going to build altars to Ashtoreth, nor are they going to worship Zeus or Artemis, if they make a decision to marry non-Christians or those who make only the flimsiest of a Christian confession. Yet this should not lead us to suppose that the problem of incompatibility or the danger of corruption has now decreased. Idols exist in different forms: alien modes of thought, competing ideologies, humanistic patterns of life and conduct, people and things that claim supreme allegiance, standards that do not conform to the revealed will and way of God for his people. Christians who willingly and wittingly enter into "foreign" marriages still run the risk of both unbearable strain and open or insidious relapse into a modern form of idolatry, nor have they any claim upon God for help in resisting the almost inevitable pressures that ensue. God may be gracious. He may not only defend his servant but bring the unconverted partner to repentance and faith. But he has given no promise to do this. The Spirit directs Christians to Christian marriages, not to mixed marriages with non-Christians.

A fourth direction of the Spirit has to do with Christian marriage itself. Two points are included here. First, marriage is good. Hebrews puts this forthrightly: "Let marriage be held in honor among all" (13:4a). Part of this honoring consists in keeping the marriage bed undefiled and avoiding adultery (13:4b). In the situation after the fall Paul discerns an additional and more negative reason for marriage: "Because of the temptation to immorality, each man should have his own wife and each woman her own husband" (1 Cor. 7:2). Yet marriage is not merely a safety valve. It is good in itself and may well be God's choice for individual Christians. Those who are unmarried should not avoid marriage on the false assumption that there is at root something wrong with it and that celibacy is intrinsically a higher and better way. "Each has his own special gift from God" (7:7) and those who do not have the gift of celibacy and cannot exercise self-control, may certainly marry and should in fact do so (7:8). Nor should Christian husbands and wives ever feel that they ought to withhold conjugal rights from one another. They may do this by common consent for limited periods, but in marrying they have given their bodies to one another (7:3ff.). Marriage is in no sense a sin. There is no need to feel guilty about it. To marry is to do well, even though in Paul's judgment not to marry may be to do better (7:36ff.).

This leads directly to the second point. Christians should still maintain in relation to marriage that reserve which God the Son exemplifies in his own incarnate life. While marriage is good, it is not obligatory. Celibacy, too, is a live option for Christians and should be prayerfully considered and respected (1 Cor. 7:8, 25ff.). Three points may be made in its favor. First, marriage as it must be practiced even by Christians in the present world-order carries with it additional secular burdens and concerns which they can well do without (7:28ff.). Second, the coming of Christ will shortly end the present order, so that even those who have wives and husbands must live as though they did not, i.e., they must live out their lives here with the perspective of eternity, when the form of this world will have gone and marriage itself will go with it (7:29ff.). As we have seen, this does not mean that husbands and

58

wives should practice constant celibacy within marriage (7:3ff.). It means, rather, that they should not absolutize marriage nor anything else that belongs to this passing order. Important though they may be, these matters are no longer of all-consuming importance, for they are relativized by the new order which Christ's coming will shortly initiate. Third, unmarried men and women are free from the cares and attachments of the married and can thus give themselves with greater devotion to the Lord and the things of the Lord (7:32ff.). Other people, relationships, and things can, of course, divert Christians from full commitment to Christ. But marriage might well be described as the most intimate and demanding of all human commitments. Hence the possibility of a clash or division of interests is especially high at this point. (This is a reason why mixed marriages are so particularly dangerous. When Christian partners share a Christian commitment, the danger is obviously lessened.) The married, who are tempted to put husband and wife or children first, find greater difficulty in achieving the primary commitment to Christ which lies at the very heart of faith and discipleship. The apostle makes it clear, of course, that the difficulty is not insuperable. He does not want to enforce celibacy on any Christian; he merely points out why it is an option—a higher one for some believers—that deserves consideration.

A fifth direction of the Spirit relates to the mutual obligations of husbands and wives. Three passages deal with these: Ephesians 5:21ff., Colossians 3:18f., and 1 Peter 3:1-7. Developed in these portions of scripture are four main points which are all important for Christian marriage if it is to be lived in the power of the Holy Spirit as part of the new life in Jesus Christ.

First, all Christians, whether male or female, share equally in the gift of salvation and eternal life that comes through Jesus Christ. Husbands and wives, as Peter beautifully phrases it, are joint heirs of the grace of life (3:7). In God's kingdom marriage yields to an even higher and deeper relationship into which Christians have already entered and in which sexual distinction makes no difference. On earth, of course, differences such as those that may be traced to sex remain in force. For Christians, however, they have only relative and temporary significance, not absolute and eternal. They are to be seen always in the light of the common calling and inheritance.

Second, husbands and wives both fall under the supreme principle of Christian life, i.e., that of service. Christ himself, the head of the church, did not come "to be served but to serve, and to give his life as a ransom for many" (Matt. 20:28). All his followers, no matter who or what they are in secular life, are pledged to the same course. Neither in relation to God nor to one another can they claim the power or privilege of rule. If they want to be great, they can be so only by rendering service to others (Matt. 20:26ff.). As Ephesians so aptly puts it, husbands and wives must be "subject to one another out of reverence for Christ" (5:21).

Third, differentiation still occurs within the common salvation and the mutual service. Christians still live in this world. The distinctions of this world and of life in this world are not obliterated. Men and women are all one in Christ and husband and wife are pledged to mutual service, but men are still men and women women, husbands are still husbands and wives wives. Freedom of sex does not consist of trying to be what one is not. Within marriage the differentiation of men and women, or husbands and wives, takes the form of order, of an ordered equality in which there is no superiority or inferiority but in which one is first and the other second. All the relevant passages make this point. According to Ephesians 5:23f., the husband is the head of the wife and the wife is to be subject to her husband. According to Colossians 3:18, wives are to be subject to their husbands. According to 1 Peter 3:1ff., wives are to be submissive to their husbands. Difficulties arise within this order only because the old Adam and old Eve still assert themselves to break up the harmony in which the wills of marriage partners coincide and headship and subjection represent no threat to equality. When a clash of wills occurs, either through the unreasonable and unjustifiable demands of the husband or through the self-will and rebelliousness of the wife, headship seems to be tyranny and subjection seems to be servitude, so that conflict results. But the point of the gospel is the reconciliation of wills, first of our wills with God's will and then of our wills with the wills of others within the common reconciliation with God's will. In calling for headship and submission, the direction of the Spirit is neither endorsing tyranny nor enjoining servitude. It is directing to the new life of Christ in which differentiation remains but only on the premise of reconciliation with God, of equality of salvation and service, and of mutual forgiveness and discipleship. It is a direction to order, but to an order of equality and love.

Fourth, the direction indicates that while husband and wife serve one another, different aspects of service are to be stressed in the light of the ongoing distinction. The husband is especially to love his wife. He must do this as he loves his own body. This means that he is to nourish and cherish her (Eph. 5:28f.). Love of this kind excludes harshness (Col. 3:19). On the positive side, it demands considerateness (1 Pet. 3:7). It also means that honor must be shown to the wife *(loc. cit.)*. In her position as the equal second partner in marriage, she is to be accorded full dignity by her husband, as the equal first partner. The wife for her part should express her love by showing to her husband the subjection which denotes respect (Eph. 5:22, cf. Col. 3:18). The reverent and chaste behavior of the wife commends the gospel, and God values highly the inner adornment of a gentle and quiet spirit (1 Pet. 3:1ff.). The final recommendation in 1 Peter 3:6, like the initial one in 3:1f., suggests that this aspect of the direction applies particularly to wives who have been converted but whose husbands are still non-Christians. These wives have a chance to win their husbands to faith, but they will do so best, not by bossing or nagging them, but by showing forth the servant-spirit of Christ in their lives. When they do this, they certainly will not need to be afraid, no matter how difficult the situation might be. In similar testimony to the gospel, Titus 2:4f. recommends that younger wives be taught to love their husbands and to express this love by being sensible, chaste, domestic, kind, and submissive. Young men, for their part, should give evidence of their love by the exercise of self-control (2:6).

It has sometimes been suggested, especially in more recent times, that the details of this fifth direction apply only to the first recipients of the epistles and to those who live within similar secular structures. These people were and are to express their mutual love and service as husbands and wives in accordance with the roles that their societies allot to the different partners in marriage. In other times and places the partners may have different roles and in such cases, while the general direction is still valid, the wife may have to nourish and cherish the husband, the husband may have to be submissive to the wife, or, if a situation of legal and social equality has been attained, neither need be submissive to the other. Discussion of this view at the deeper theological level must be postponed until the next section, but in the meantime some general observations may be helpful. First, the direction itself does not indicate that either it or its details apply only to specific people in a specific sociological context. Second, there is no apparent reason why only the details, or only this direction, or only marital teaching should come under this form of relativizing and not many other matters, both doctrinal and practical, in which the words or thought-forms of a given age or structure are employed — so long as this principle of relativizing has any validity. But has it? This leads on to the next point. Third, sociological contexts, whether ancient or modern, have nowhere been sanctified by the divine Word and Spirit as standards by which to determine the right forms of the expression of Christian love and service in any given age or place. God establishes his own standards which will usually bring sociological structures under serious scrutiny and incisive criticism. Fourth, details of this direction call for specific conduct by husbands and wives which cuts right across all sociological patterns, rebuking them but also being for them a sign of the reconciliation of God and his new work of creation. Fifth, relativizing the divine direction by secular structures of human life puts things the wrong way round; the true relativizing is that of all secular structures, which know little of true equality, order, or service, by the divine direction. Christian husbands and wives of all ages and places are summoned, then, constructively to adopt and follow the fifth direction both in general and in detail, no matter whether they live in a patriarchal, matriarchal, egalitarian, or any other society.

A sixth direction of the Spirit firmly endorses the teaching of Jesus that Christian marriage be permanent. Paul states this very clearly and categorically in 1 Corinthians 7:10f.: "The wife should not separate from her husband (but if she does, let her remain single or else be reconciled to her husband) — and that the husband should not divorce his wife." Behind this direction stands the authority of the Lord: "I give charge, not I but the Lord." The injunction thus repeats and interprets Christ's own saying about divorce in the Gospels. The concession of the Mosaic law no longer applies to husbands. Husbands may not divorce their wives any more than wives may leave their husbands. If they do, they are not to remarry. The door of reconciliation must be left open. Implicitly if not explicitly, remarriage by either partner in the case of separation is viewed as adultery. In the new life in Christ which Christians may live by the power of the Spirit, the original intention of marriage — the indissoluble union of one man and one woman — is now to be achieved as God's children refashion their attitudes and affections and acts in conformity with the enacted will of God in his own convenantal dealings with them. The one exception will be discussed in the next section.

A seventh and final direction offers special instruction to the bishops (presbyters) and deacons of the church. Both the bishop (1 Tim. 3:2; Tit. 1:6) and the deacon (1 Tim. 3:12) must be the husband of one wife. The precise meaning of this direction has given rise to much debate. It can hardly be adduced in favor of the compulsory celibacy that some churches have imposed on their clergy! Nor does it seem to have in view compulsory marriage; it is not insisting that every bishop or deacon be the husband of one wife. Undoubtedly, it forbids polygamy, although whether this was a live issue at the time of writing is perhaps open to question. It would also seem to exclude remarrying after divorce. This would be ruled out, of course, by the sixth direction, but the seventh might be formulated with a view to recent converts who had already remarried after divorce and who might not be regarded as suitable for ordination, even though they could be readily welcomed into the congregation. Another possibility is a prohibition of remarriage after the death of a former wife. Here again, since other passages do not exclude such remarriage, we might have a special rule for ordained ministers, perhaps based upon Paul's teaching about celibacy in 1 Corinthians 7:32ff. In the light of the general approach to remarriage after the dissolving of a marriage by death, however, this is by no means certain. Whatever the precise reference may be, the direction incontestably requires that ministers, by having only one wife living at a time, should set for all others an example of a solid and lasting marital commitment. Christians who fail in this regard are not necessarily debarred from the church any more than those who do not meet the other qualifications for ministry. But they should not be considered for ordination as bishops or deacons.

2. THE SOLUTIONS OF THE SPIRIT

In addition to his clear directions, the Holy Spirit offers us solutions to two problems in which different and equally legitimate courses seem to present themselves according to different circumstances. These solutions recognize that what may be best in one case may not be best in another, so that no hard and fast rules can be laid down. Nevertheless, as solutions of the Spirit, they have the authority which goes with all the words and acts of God.

The first problem has to do with marriage after the death of a first partner. We have touched on this question already in the directions of the previous section. The special direction to ministers might have this matter in view. Paul is certainly talking about remarriage as well as (and perhaps more than) marriage in 1 Corinthians 7. Is it permissable that Christians should take another wife or husband when the first one dies? If it is permissible, is it advisable?

The question of permissibility can be answered very quickly. Paul, in Romans 7:1ff., points out that marital commitments, like all other legal ties, cease with death. Thus a married person commits adultery if he or she lives with another while the first partner is still alive. When the first partner dies, however, the one who is left may marry another without being guilty of adultery. No obstacle to a second marriage exists once death breaks the original bond. On one interpretation, as we have seen, a second marriage after the death of a first wife might be forbidden to bishops and deacons. In view of the general permissibility of such a marriage, however, it hardly seems likely that this is the correct interpretation of this special direction.

The second question, that of advisability, cannot be answered so easily. On the one hand, Paul says clearly that it is better for widows and widowers, as well as for the unmarried, to remain single, as he himself does (1 Cor. 7:8). (Whether Paul ranks as a bachelor or as a widower is an intriguing question that has led to much discussion and speculation but cannot be answered with final certainty.) On the other hand, it has to be remembered that

Paul also states that not all people have the divine gift of self-control which is needed if they are to remain celibate. Those who do not have the gift obviously commit no offense by remarrying. "If the husband dies, a wife is free to be married to whom she wishes" (so long as it is "in the Lord," 7:39). The same applies to the husband. Nevertheless, Paul believes that the Holy Spirit supports him when he adds that, all things considered, "she [or he] is happier if she remains as she is" (7:40).

This might seem to be the end of the matter. It is not. Remarriage can, after all, be the better course in certain circumstances. Widows in particular often need financial help and the burden of providing this can fall on the congregations. Older widows, of course, can often render useful services (1 Tim. 5:3, 9ff.)—so much so that a kind of order of widows seems to have existed in the early church (1 Tim. 5:9, 11) — but younger widows can become a problem. They do not all achieve the singlehearted devotion to the Lord which is one of the chief reasons for remaining single. They have a tendency to fall into idle and gossipy ways which do more to bring the gospel into disrepute than to commend it. Out of a desire for marriage they may go back on their commitment to congregational service in a certain disloyalty to Christ. They do better, then, to remarry and raise families (1 Tim. 5:11ff.), in spite of the general ruling of the apostle that the widow is happier if she remains as she is.

Whether or not the same situation might arise with widowers is hard to say. Normally they would be less likely to need financial support, so that from this angle they do not come under the same pressure to remarry. On the other hand, the desire to marry again might be present and might lead to unsuitable conduct if it is not met. There is certainly no reason why it should not be met, as is clear from the discussion in 1 Corinthians 7. If the direction to bishops and deacons to have only one wife is a direction against remarriage, this might mean that widowers, like widows, are particularly suitable for ordination because they do not have to meet the rival claims of family life. On the other hand, since bishops and deacons are also to rule their own households well, it is obvious that office-bearers do not heave to be celibates or widowers (1 Tim. 3:4, 12).

In many parts of the world today widows are no longer dependent on congregational support as they were in the primitive church. They can either earn their own living or receive help from systems of social welfare. Since scripture itself seems specifically to have the economic background in view, they would thus seem to be in essentially the same position as widowers, free to remarry if there is the desire or urge to do so, but not under obligation to adopt the solution proposed for younger widows in other circumstances. In other places, however, where widows do not yet enjoy this economic freedom, the valid recommendation of 1 Timothy might still be the better course for them.

The second problem is that of marriages that are mixed because of the conversion of one of the partners after the marriage was contracted. The husband or wife becomes a Christian but not the other partner. Here is a situation that differs completely from the marriage of an existing Christian with a non-Christian. In this instance the mixed marriage comes about coincidentally, not intentionally. How is a Christian to act in such circumstances?

It might be noted that in the apostolic age the problem is normally more acute for the wife than for the husband. The husband may, if he chooses, impose his religious beliefs and practices, at least externally, on his wife and his household in general. The wife has to be more circumspect, as may be seen from 1 Peter 3:1ff. She may not have the approval of her husband either for her conversion to Christ or for the life of renewal that is hers in him. Nevertheless, the husband does not escape the problem. Even if external compliance is forced on the wife, it may go hand in hand with deep-seated opposition that can make life very difficult and that may even lead to the wife's termination of the marriage. In other ages and places, of course, the husband has no particular legal advantage in matters of faith. Hence the solutions proposed by the Spirit apply in measure to both husbands and wives.

First, the believing partner should not take any initiative toward separation from the unbelieving partner (1 Cor. 7:12f.) The principle of separation that underlies the direction to Christians not to marry pagans has no relevance to this situation. "Foreign" wives had to be put away in post-exilic Israel, but in that case members of the holy people had deliberately entered into union with them, often divorcing their true wives to do so. Here, however, both partners are at first "foreigners." One of them, hearing the gospel and accepting it, becomes a member of the household of faith. This does not make the marriage sinful. If the pagan wife or husband consents to continue living with the converted partner, then the Christian must not seek separation. The Spirit rules against this. To seek the termination of the marriage would now be the sin.

Second, if the pagan partner is willing that the marriage should go on, the believer has the assurance of at least a possibility of winning the pagan to faith in Christ (1 Cor. 7:14). No promise of any kind, of course, is held out when believers willingly and wittingly marry pagans. But here the believing partner brings a certain "consecration" or "holiness" to the unbelieving partner and to any children of the marriage. By the faith of the one, the others are set in a special sphere. A witness can be given, not least of all by conduct that commends the gospel, which may lead to the winning of those who do not yet obey the word (1 Pet. 3:1f.). The tentative encouragement is given: "Wife, how do you know whether you will save your husband? Husband, how do you know whether you will save your wife?" (1 Cor. 7:16). The bearing of Christian witness, which is also given by doing everything possible to uphold the marriage, constitutes a dominant concern in this whole matter. To bear this witness Christians have to live their life of renewal as well as talk about it. They do this by being Christian in their marital relationship, difficult though this may be where the other partner does not share or even perhaps care for the Christian commitment. This is the solution that the Spirit proposes.

Third, the unconverted spouse might not consent to continue the marriage with the converted husband or wife. He or she wishes to end the union and acts to do so either by separation or desertion. When this happens, the marriage will have to end. The Christian partner can do no more. There is no way in which he or she can force the non-Christian to continue a relationship that the latter is resolved to terminate. Here, then, is a permissible exception to the strong prohibition of the dissolution of marriage both in the teaching of Jesus and in the directions of the Holy Spirit. This exception is not a concession to hardness of heart on the part of believers. It is an acceptance of the dissolution which is forced on believers by hardness of heart on the part of their non-Christian partners. Disciples have here no control over the divorce.

They do not wish it and they have no responsibility for it. It may be freely stated, then, that "in such a case the brother or sister is not bound" (1 Cor. 7:15).

This acceptance of dissolution when an unbelieving husband or wife refuses to live on with a converted partner raises the broader question of whether the exception applies only in this particular case or whether it offers a model for other exceptions in other peculiar circumstances. One might think of some close parallels, e.g., when a believing partner renounces the faith and then repudiates his or her marriage with another believer. Or one might think of less analogous situations where, e.g., a believing partner runs off adulterously with another person or behaves in a totally unchristian way so that continued life in concert becomes impossible. One might also think of instances in which, e.g., incest or bigamy is discovered, or a spouse is completely incapacitated or alienated by physical or mental illness, or problems of adjustment prove to be too serious for a successful relationship. Once one considers the position that the permission of 1 Corinthians 7 might be a kind of blank check to be filled out as individual situations suggest, there is hardly any end to the extension of possibilities.

It is probably wisest, however, to treat the scriptural solution as simply a solution to the scriptural problem. The problem will never cease to arise so long as the church is doing the evangelistic and missionary work that it is commissioned to do. Conversion and allegiance to Christ can very well cause breakups of marriages and families in which the new and higher commitment cannot surrender to the older and lower but must try to work with it and within it. If the unconverted partner will not accept this but terminates the marriage, then the believer has the justification, not of some pleaded innocence in a messy relation, but of the right of the higher allegiance and of faithfulness to it.

In other circumstances believers may not be able to prevent the dissolution of marriage by other believing but apostate, adulterous, unsanctified, or incompatible partners. But the dissolution is wrong because it runs counter to the direction of the Spirit, and two wrongs will not make a right. Believers do not in such circumstances have to accept the new and non-biblical situation that is thrust upon them and abandon their own faithfulness to the covenanted marriage. A readiness for reconciliation may be one-sided, as God's was with Israel, but so long as the door stays open a response can still come from the other side as the Spirit works to bring the erring believer to repentance for the fault that has brought disruption. If the readiness for reconciliation makes a stern demand, this, after all, is what being a disciple is all about. Christian conduct exacts a price from us as God's atoning work exacted a price from him. Grace practiced as well as grace received is not cheap.

The same cost has to be faced when incapacity strikes a partner in marriage. Now, above all, is the time for the new quality of love, or the quality of the new love, to shine forth. Now, above all, the rule of mutual service makes an ultimate demand for unselfish commitment which entails no getting for giving but only giving. This lies at the very heart of the marital union as it lies at the very heart of the divine union with us. The marital union has many facets, including the delights of sexual love and the joy of shared experiences and companionship. Its final authenticity, however, is that of holding fast when disaster strikes. Compassionate perseverence in love is what really counts.

Naturally, circumstances arise when separation may be advisable and even necessary. Christians, too, can be or become cruel and vindictive and physically or mentally dangerous. Yet even though the victim may have little or no control over events in this unhappy situation, there is no ground for dissolution of the bond of marriage as in desertion by an unconverted partner. Here is no unbeliever but a confessing believer who is seriously failing to die to sin and live to God, or who has fallen prey to sickness of mind and who still needs the help of prayer and of openness to reconciliation, even though this help can be given only at heavy cost. The comparatively easy escape of remarriage, which rules out all hope of reconciliation on the basis of future repentance and renewal, runs contrary to the direction of the Spirit and can appeal only improperly to the freedom permitted by the Spirit in the case of pagan desertion.

Nullification of a marriage, it would seem, can still take place should suitable grounds be present. Some of these, such as incest, bigamy, or marriage based on deliberate deception, raise few problems. Others are more debatable, even after centuries of discussion. In this area, too, one must avoid a blank check mentality which simply sees a line that only has to be filled out in some way to justify a dissolution. If a few marriages should never have been begun, the vast majority should not be ended except by death. The Holy Spirit through scripture does not in fact give explicit guidance on nullification. One can proceed only by noting what things, being either prohibited or totally incompatible with marriage, make a marriage intrinsically impossible from the very outset. In debatable matters, no matter how they may be decided, it must never be forgotten that the Spirit urges upon Christians a high commitment to marriage, within the higher commitment to Christ, which the church should be happy to accept and uphold.

3. THE CHRISTOLOGICAL WITNESS OF THE SPIRIT

The commitment to marriage, as we have just noted, lies within the higher commitment to Christ. It also rests upon it. For commitment to Christ forms the basis of commitment to marriage. Or perhaps this should be put the other way round. Christ's own commitment to his people forms the basis of their commitment to one another in marriage (as indeed in all their relationships). The Holy Spirit, whose function it is to bear witness to Christ (John 16:14), shows how this is so. What might appear in themselves to be quasi-legalistic directions or casuistic solutions to specific problems take on a wholly new appearance, or are seen to have a different dimension, when their christological foundation is brought to light. The concern for marriage derives both primarily and finally from a concern for Christ's relation to his people. The form and nature of marriage reflect the form and nature of this prior, original, and controlling union.

Of the two chief New Testament passages which present the Spirit's christological witness, the first may be found in 1 Corinthians 11. It occurs in the unlikely setting of a discussion of the wearing of a headcovering by women believers when they engage in praying or prophesying. Apparently some of the women in Corinth were setting aside the practice, or at least contesting it, and the apostle seized the occasion to give reasons for what might seem in itself to be a custom of little significance.

Primarily the headcovering seems to have served as a differentiating mark. Women were to wear it while men were not. Differentiation does not mean discrimination in the pejorative sense. While men and women are all one in Christ Jesus (Gal. 3:28), their equality in faith does not terminate their sexual distinction. A relation exists between them, and especially between husband and wife, in which they are "ordered" to one another. Within the unity in Christ the husband is the head of the wife, not *vice versa*. The covered and uncovered heads denote this order.

What the order entails is not left to speculation but is brought out in the course of the apostolic discussion. We may mention first an important recollection of the creation story. According to God's action in creation, it is man (the male) who is primarily God's image and glory. Woman, too, is made in God's image, but she is God's glory secondarily as the glory of man (1 Cor. 11:7). The reason for this is that man was made first and then woman was made out of man and for man, not man out of woman and for woman (11:8). Lest this should seem to imply inequality, Paul is careful to add that even though woman was originally made from man, man is no less dependent on her than she on him, for man is now born of woman. The true primacy and only real supremacy rest with God, who is the source of both man and woman: "All things are from God" (11:11f.). Only under this divine primacy and supremacy does man have the primacy of order. But under this primacy and supremacy he does have it.

Significant though all this is, however, it is in fact only a supporting thesis. The truth and basis of the man/woman (or husband/wife) relationship rest and are to be sought in Christ himself. It is here at the heart of the matter that Paul himself begins, only later going on to deal with the secondary consideration from creation, and then finally with the ancillary teaching of nature (11:13-15).

Christ, first of all, has a downward relationship to man in which he is the head of man: "The head of every man is Christ" (11:3). If we think of man here as every man, whether Christian or not, this does not imply radical inequality, for, although Christ is the divine Son, in virtue of the incarnation he is also man among men. So far as Christians are concerned, equality also exists inasmuch as they are members of the church, which in virtue of the divine marriage is now one body with Christ. Yet there is differentiation too. One cannot reverse the statement that Christ is man and say that man is Christ. While true man, Christ is also true God; this can be said of no other man. Even as man, Christ has priority over all other men. He might be called the primal man or the prototype of man, for it is in his image that we are being newly created and to his image that we are being conformed. Similarly, while Christian man is a member of the body of Christ, only of Christ himself can it be said that he is the head of the body. Differentiated or ordered equality characterizes the relation between Christ and man which scripture proposes as a model for the relation between man and woman (or husband and wife).

Christ also stands in an upward relationship and this time the roles are reversed, for while Christ is the head of man the Father is the head of Christ: "And the head of Christ is God" (11:3). From what we read elsewhere in scripture this relationship as well entails no inequality. Father and Son are coequally God. Again, however, it involves an ordered differentiation. Within the unity of the triune being God the Father is not the Son nor the Son the Father. When Paul says that the head of Christ is God, we have another irreversible statement. One could not say that the head of God, or even the head of the Father, is Christ. Quite apart from the incarnation, in which the incarnate Son subjects himself to the will of the Father, the Father comes first and the Son second. The Father, as the fount of deity, eternally begets the Son. Differentiated or ordered equality again characterizes the relation which serves as a further model for the relation between man and woman (and husband and wife).

Two points should be noted. Paul does not tidily arrange the three relationships in an ascending or descending hierarchical order, as some of his commentators are tempted to do. We do not read that the head of Christ is God, the head of every man is Christ, and the head of woman is man, as though we had some kind of chain of authority or command. Nor does the list work upward from man as the head of woman to Christ as the head of man to God as the head of Christ, as though we were gradually moving from lesser centers of authority to the highest center. Paul begins, as it were, in the middle of any such series with the man as the head of the woman. This is the point at issue and it finds both illustration and confirmation in the two fundamental relationships of the whole teaching of scripture: the intratrinitarian relationship of the Father and Son and the christological and ecclesiological relationship of Christ and humanity and Christ and the new humanity, the church.

Second, the ordered equality of man and woman finds a special application in marriage, and particularly in Christian marriage, as the detailed directions for husbandly and wifely service indicate. The passage in 1 Corinthians 11 makes no direct reference to the marriage of Christ and the church, nor does it address the question of the specific ministries of husbands and wives, for, after all, the point at issue is that of headcovering as a mark of general sexual differentiation. Nevertheless, the relation between Christ and his bride, which is delineated more particularly in Ephesians 5, stands indirectly in the background. So, too, does the relation between husband and wife. A successful union may be attained, in the power of the Holy Spirit, when husband and wife, not with a sense of duty or obligation, but freely, spontaneously, and cheerfully, model their fulfilment of mutual marital service on the ordered equality whereby man is the head of woman as Christ is head of his people and God is the head of Christ. Nor will Christian man and woman see any urgent reason to make an issue of the matter — few men and relatively few women have ever done so throughout Christian history — if some token of their relation, as that of God to Christ and Christ to man, is given in the exercise of prayer and prophecy.

Ephesians 5:21ff., to which reference has just been made, is the second passage which offers a christological model for Christian marriage. These verses, too, command a structural relationship in which husband and wife, each subject to the other, discharge their mutual ministries in different ways. In the depiction of these different forms of service the primary reference is to Christ and his church. The closing verses, however, make it clear that the union of Christ and the church is the union of Christ and his bride, in which the two become one (5:31f.). On the human side the author is directly and explicitly dealing with the relationship of man and woman in marriage.

The passage makes a series of important affirmations about Christ and the church. It first describes Christ as "the head of the church, his body" (5:23). This headship does not imply any separation of being, as though the church had a head apart from itself. The head is part of the body and the church as a body is Christ's body. The headship is thus exercised within unity. At the same time, it is real headship, for the body is subject to the head, not superior to it or independent of it. Like Christ and the church, husband and wife are one body, so that in their relationship of head and body there can be no question of separate and competing beings, as in the poor attempts at marriage of which even Christians are so often guilty when they fail to live out their new life to God in the power of the Holy Spirit. The relation between head and body has to be a relation within the union. Within the union, however, it is very distinctly a relation of head and body, each in service of the other.

The passage then affirms that Christ is Savior and that in his love he gave himself up as such (5:23, 25). He did this in order that he might sanctify and cleanse the church and thus present it to himself in unblemished perfection. Here, of course, the analogy to human marriage breaks down, for both husband and wife need Christ as Savior and depend on his love and self-sacrifice, his sanctifying and cleansing work. In this regard they stand together within the church as the body or bride of Christ. Nevertheless, the analogy does not break down totally. Christ offers himself as a model for the husband, at least within the sphere of the latter's competence. The husband should display the same unselfish love as Christ displayed in his saving work. Assuming responsibility for the welfare of his wife, he should love and care for her as for himself: "He who loves his wife loves himself" (5:28), for in marriage they become one. The love of the divine husband for his bride can still offer a powerful example to the human husband. This love alone, the love of care and forgiveness and reconciliation and faithfulness and self-giving, is what marriage is all about. Similarly, as the church responds to Christ with its devotion and consecration and service, so the wife can and should respond to her husband with a similar ministry of love and care and compassion and concern. Even in the best of Christian marriages, in which there is an earnest resolve to live the new life and a willing openness to the enlightening and empowering ministry of the Spirit, strains and stresses will constantly arise which necessitate this ministry of love if the marriage is not just to survive but to be the kind of marriage that God desires. So long as life lasts on earth, marriage will be that of sinners in a sinful world. But as the marriage of pardoned sinners it can also be a mutual ministry of caring love. This will be its strongest safeguard against the divisive and destructive forces of human waywardness and weakness.

Finally, the passage affirms the unity of Christ and his body in terms which clearly indicate marriage. As God said of man and woman at the first, "They become one flesh," so through the apostle he says of Christ and the church, "The two shall be one" (5:31). God himself in his marriage with his people fulfils the kind of marital union which God the Creator proclaims and God the Son clearly and firmly proclaims again. Here is an intimate and indissoluble union in which each loves and cares for the other because each is joined and united to the other, the church as the body of Christ and Christ as the head (and indeed the whole body, 1 Cor. 12:4ff.) of the church. As with Christ and his bride, so also with the husband and wife: they, too, can really become one. Because Christ by his saving work has provided the new possibility, and the Holy Spirit with his power has opened the door to its actualization, they can love one another with a wholehearted commitment, an unselfish concern, a forgiving grace, and an unflagging faithfulness. They themselves are being refashioned in the image of Christ, which involves a restoration of the original creation in the image of God. So, too, their marriage can be refashioned in the image of Christ's marriage, which means the restoration of marriage to the original pattern and intent of the Creator.

In this christological grounding of marriage, in which our marriage reflects Christ's marriage, the latter, of course, is the one that has eternal and eschatological significance. Did not the Lord himself teach us that in his kingdom there will be no marriage or giving in marriage at our human level? With the ending of the age, earthly marriage will end too, just as death already can part those who are united in it. Christ's marriage, however, will go on into the new and eternal age. Only then, indeed, will it come to its full and final fulfilment: "For the marriage of the Lamb has come, and his bride has made herself ready" (Rev. 19:7). Here is the ultimate and definitive relationship in which husbands and wives who are members of Christ's church, and therefore one with Christ in his body, find the perfect completion of their own relationship. Between the ascension of Christ and his coming again, earthly marriages can be reconstituted and reconstructed. They can reflect and bear witness to the divine marriage in which they have their source and from which they draw their strength. They can achieve a measure of temporal durability and depth. They can offer a foretaste of the renewed and perfected relationship in Christ which is known in part on earth but will come to its full fruition in the life to come. But eventually they must end. They must give place to the eternally enduring marriage of God and his people in which God has brought his gracious purpose to completion and his people has been fully reclaimed and regenerated and renewed. It is of this marriage that Christian marriage is in its halting way a prophetic sign. It is to this marriage as a divine prototype that it aspires as a human copy. It is in this marriage that it finds the totality of what it can now achieve only partially and progressively. This is the marriage which is its basis, meaning, and goal.

Conclusion

W HAT is the upshot of all this? Does it help at all in the practice of married life? Have we simply climbed a lofty theological peak which offers an excellent view but is remote from the realities of marriage and the problems that afflict those who are trying to make a success of it? Or can the biblical picture, with its sober realism as well as its lofty understanding, bring us genuine help — the type of help that nothing else can finally offer — in making marriage the kind of union that it may and can and should be? And if so, how?

The first step we must take if we are to receive the help that a biblical view can surely give, is not merely to see but authentically to understand that marriage has a christological original, basis, and starting-point. In creating man—male and female—in his own image, and joining them together so that they become one flesh, God makes us copies both of himself in his trinitarian unity and distinction as one God and three persons and of himself in relation to the people of his gracious election. Analogically, what is between Father, Son, and Holy Spirit, and what ought to be and is and shall be between God and Israel and Christ and the church, is also what is meant to be in the relation of man and woman and more specifically of husband and wife. Neither the intratrinitarian relationship nor the union between the heavenly bridegroom and his bride is a good copy of a bad original. Earthly marriage as it is now lived out is a bad copy of a good original.

The copy became a bad one because man and woman distorted the original relation by living to self instead of living to God. Falling away from God meant falling out with one another. They could not even see the original of their special relationship any more. They substituted a version of their own which, while it necessarily retained traces of what God intended, since they could not cease to be the creatures that God had made, introduced such factors as selfishness, arrogance, greed, violence, and deceit which made even the maintenance of a marital relation difficult, let alone its happy and harmonious functioning. To perceive where the real problem lies, forms an essential part of the process of healing. Within a given marriage immediate and individual difficulties arise which may be resolved by psychological techniques or good advice or resolves to do better. Fundamentally, however, marriage cannot be set on a truly solid basis unless (a) the original relation of both man and woman to God is set right and (b) this restored relation becomes the form according to which all human relations, including that of marriage, are reconstituted and reformed. If marriage is to enjoy a measure of success, or of successful repair, we have to put it in the perspective not only of its divine original but also of the divine restoration of the underlying marriage between God and us.

This is not, of course, as simple as it all sounds. Or perhaps it is really much simpler. Difficulty arises because people so easily begin to think that God provides us with an example that we then have the task of following. They quickly find that they have no power of their own to restore the original relation to God or even properly to understand it. God himself in grace does, and has to do, this work of enlightenment and restitution. But even when the work is done and they understand the relation and enter into it, they cannot transpose it into the realities of everyday relationships with one another, especially in marriage. This is why it is not as simple as it sounds.

It is simpler, however, because God himself took the initiative at the level of both original and copy. At the level of the original the deserted husband lovingly went to look for the erring bride and bought her back. He did this by offering himself, in the person of the divine Son, as the price of redemption. He paid the debt, bore the sin, wiped out the guilt, and in an incomparable display of gracious love restored the marriage on a new and eternal basis, making it possible for his bride to respond with the love of gratitude and faith and adoration. By God's action we may thus enter again into the relationship which we broke and find in it, or more specifically find in the action of the heavenly bridegroom and the response that it evokes, the original of which our human marriage is now to be the copy.

At the level of the copy, God the Holy Spirit grants newness of life in Christ to those who are thus restored to fellowship with God, so that they, too, can love as God did and does. In need of God's salvation, they see also their need in relation to one another. Forgiven, they learn to forgive and to seek forgiveness. Taught by the self-sacrificing love of Christ, they discover what true love is. They do all this slowly and with difficulty. The sinner in them does not want to let go. Left to their own resources they could not do it, even with the splendid example of God and the powerful motivation of gratitude. Words and thoughts and acts of cruelty and insensitivity and division and resentment and self-centeredness would constantly stand in the way. Marriages would still crumble under the weight of cumulative perversion. But what Christians cannot do on their own, they can do with the power of the Holy Spirit. The Holy Spirit will not let them fall. He will bring them back again and again for divine forgiveness and restoration. He will convict them of their sins and failures. He will strengthen them through the word and sacrament and prayer and fellowship. He will point them to the Christ in whom they believe and on whom they depend. He will renew them so that in spite of themselves they may achieve a faithful, steadfast, concerned, forgiving, and serving love in place of what could so easily be no more than the shallow and shoddy sinners' love that cannot stand the harsh test of human reality.

At both levels, then, the way to the establishment or restoration of authentic marriage may be described as simple. It is the soteriological way, the way of divine salvation. God himself has done what is necessary to achieve his primary purpose of fellowship between himself and us. In so doing he has also done what is necessary for us to achieve the human copy of the divine original. By the vicarious work of the divine Son and the indwelling ministry of the divine Spirit the Father has opened the way for the fulfilment of human marriage within the triumphant consolidation of the divine marriage.

What we must do, as the second step, is to accept the twofold work of God — his work for us and his work in us — in a commitment of faith and obedience and prayer. This demands an element of decision. Do we want this work of God or do we prefer our own? Do we want God's will to be done on earth, or do we want to do our own will? We are not to decide abstractly. This decision reaches into all the concrete situations of life. It reaches into our marriage. Do we want the will of God to be done in our marriage or do we want to do our own will? Do we want the work of God whereby he restores our relationship to himself and thereby revolutionizes our relationship in marriage or do we want our own work? God has canceled the past. He has made it possible for us to love as he has loved us, to be faithful to one another as he has been faithful to us, to be patient and forbearing as he has been, to forgive as he has forgiven, to be ready to serve as he has served. He will help us to fight and defeat everything in us that resists this. But do we want his help and enabling? Even as those who believe in Christ and accept the reconciliation with God that he has achieved for us, are we ready to be real Christians who are similarly reconciled to one another, who are dead to sin and alive to God, who aim at every point and in every situation of life to be in fact what they already are in Christ and in hope? We cannot, of course, make this decision on our own. Only God's decision for us makes it possible. But within that decision, and empowered by it, we can and must decide.

Finally, we must realize that as marriage has a christological original and a soteriological basis, so it has an eschatological goal. In a sense the original, basis, and goal are the same. The marriage of God and his people is the original. The achieving or restoring of this marriage is the basis. The glorious and eternal fulfilment of this marriage, after the episode of human desertion and reclamation, is the goal. God does not let his original purpose come to nothing. By way of the reconciling work of the Son and the regenerating ministry of the Spirit, he overcomes the threatened separation and maintains the union. In spite of all remaining opposition, he will bring his plan to joyful and victorious fulfilment when this age reaches its end and all things are definitively made new.

By relativizing earthly marriage, it might seem that the eschatological goal weakens and devalues it. If earthly marriage has no future, why should people worry about making it work or conforming it to the divine pattern? Does it matter that much if even Christian marriages, when they cause pain and strife, finally break up in disorder and failure? What do Christian achievements in this life count for if they can never be more than transitory and imperfect and will at the end be replaced by that which is perfect and eternal?

The fallacy in this type of reasoning is to assume that because the eschatological climax relativizes the human relationship, it necessarily negates it. Far from doing this, it sets the relationship in a perspective which gives it true validity and significance. Marriage has the high dignity that it does just because it is both a copy of the christological and soteriological original and a promise of the eschatological fulfilment. Here on earth, reconciled to God in Christ and empowered and impelled by the Holy Spirit, we can do what we were created to do on earth. On our human level we can achieve, at least in part, the reflection and promise of the divine relation from which we come and to which we go.

In achieving this reflection and promise we can also demonstrate it to the world. Here in Christian marriage is the relation that God planned for us. Here is the relation that our disobedience destroyed. Here is the relation that his saving work has made possible again. Here is a testimony to the divine relation from which we broke away but to which God wills to restore us. Here is a possibility, not for a few specially gifted people, but for sinners who in and of themselves really have no such possibility. Here is a living witness to the reality of God's redeeming grace and power. Here is faith, not in word only, but in action, working by love. Here is the beginning at least of the transformation which will come in fulness with the resurrection of the dead and the relationships of the life everlasting.

We can also enjoy this human reflection and promise of the divine relation. After all, harsh and cruel and painful though life in this world has been made by human wickedness and folly, God does not will that we should experience it merely as a series of trials, sorrows, and afflictions. Joy and happiness are part of God's purpose for his people in the process of restoration by mortification and renewal. These may be found specifically in God's new and reconciling work: the joy and happiness of sins forgiven, of peace with God, of entry into God's family, of individual and common meeting with God in prayer and praise, of contributing to God's work of evangelism and edification, of use of the means of grace. They may be found, too, in God's new and reconstructive work: the joy and happiness of appreciation of God's creation, of pleasure in work, of devotion to the ends of justice and human care, of the discovery of the true meaning and depth of human relationship, especially in marriage. Naturally these things are only a foretaste of the good things that God has prepared for those who love him (1 Cor. 2:9), of the time when pain and sorrow are finally banished and we know the gladness of the new creation. But they are a real foretaste. They are well worth having. God has given them to us truly to enjoy. Something is sadly amiss with Christian marriage if, for all the difficulties and problems, the partners do not find and taste this wonderfully renewed and increasing joy of relationship. Why should husbands and wives quarrel and drift apart and tear up themselves and their marriage, consoling themselves perhaps, if not with the thought of happiness with someone else, at least with that of a blissful eternity, when already here and now, as an essential part of his saving action, God offers them in their marriage as in other spheres a first installment of the felicity that is to come?

Creation has been restored by reconciliation. It will come to its final fulfilment in glorification. Between reconciliation and glorification comes regeneration and sanctification. This, too, forms part of God's purpose and work. This is what he wills and does now. This is what is being worked out in Christian marriage as well as in other areas of the Christian's life. We are all at different stages here. We may slip back as well as advance. But we cannot drop out of the program. Christ himself is being formed in the Christian husband or wife. Thus far his features may be very blurred and indistinct. They are obscured by the evil features of the man or woman for whom he died and rose but in whom the old sinner still lives on so obviously and so persistently. Nevertheless, those evil features belong to the dead past. The husband and wife, being Christians, died and rose again in Christ. By the Holy Spirit the new and Christlike features may and can and should emerge with increasing power and distinctness. They belong already to the present. They carry the promise of the future.

Indexes

I. SCRIPTURE REFERENCES

Scripture References

24:1-4	17, 31	**2 Kings**		31:33	28
25:5ff.	18	9:30ff.	25	**Lamentations**	
27:11ff.	18	11	24	1:7ff.	32
27:20	18			1:19	32
27:22f.	18	**Ezra**		3:22f.	32
		9:1	26		
Judges		10	21	**Ezekiel**	
13:2ff.	28	10:2	21	8:7ff.	33
14:1ff.	24			16:1ff.	30
14:15ff.	24	**Nehemiah**		16:8ff.	30
14:20	24	13:23ff.	21	16:14	30
15:6	24	13:26	25	16:30	30
16:1ff.	24			16:39	31
16:4ff.	24	**Psalms**		16:60	31
19-21	21	106:28ff.	20	16:63	31
21:25	21			23	31
		Proverbs		24:16	26
Ruth		3:16ff.	24	24:17f.	26
1:16	26	5:18ff.	24	34:11ff.	33
3:10f.	26	7:6ff.	24	36:26	44
4:10	26	12:4	26		
		18:22	26	**Hosea**	
1 Samuel		19:13	26	1-3:3	29
1f.	22	19:14	27	2	29
1:19ff.	28	21:19	26	2:5	30
		31:10ff.	27	2:14	30
2 Samuel		31:26	27	2:19f.	30
11:2ff.	22	31:30	27	4:16	33
11:4	22			7:8	33
11:6ff.	22	**Ecclesiastes**		7:11	33
11:27	22	9:9	27	10:1	33
12:13	27			11:1ff.	33
12:14	27	**Song of Songs**			
13	22	6:3	27	**Malachi**	
13:15	22	8:7	27	2:16	21
16ff.	23				
18:33	23	**Isaiah**		**Matthew**	
		40ff.	33	1:5	28
1 Kings		54	29, 32	1:6	28
1-2	23	54:4	32	1:18ff.	36
3:1ff.	24	54:5	29, 32	5:27	55
11	24	54:6	32	5:28	39
11:1ff.	24	54:8-10	32	5:31	44
11:4	24	62:5	32	5:31f.	43
11:5ff.	24	64:8	33	5:32	44
11:12f.	27	66:13	33	6:14f.	46
11:26-12:20	27			19:3ff.	40, 43
12	24	**Jeremiah**		19:8	44
16:31ff.	25	2:2	31	19:9	44, 45
18:17ff.	25	3:1	31	19:10	40
19:15ff.	27	3:6ff.	31	19:11f.	40
19:23f.	27	3:12	31	19:18	55
21	25	3:14	33	20:26ff.	60
21:25	25	3:15	33	20:28	60
21:27ff.	25, 27	3:20	31	22:23ff.	41
22	25	4:30	32		
		23:3	33		

84

II. BIBLICAL NAMES

III. SUBJECTS